"Neither a borrower nor
a lender be for loan
oft loses both itself and friend

Roscoe Fornells

Total Community
The Monks of Caldey Island

Roscoe Howells

First published 1975
2nd Edition 1982
3rd Edition (Revised) 1994

© Roscoe Howells

ISBN 1 85902 106 9

Printed in Wales
at the Gomer Press, Llandysul, Dyfed

For David and Angela
With many thanks for past help

CONTENTS

ACKNOWLEDGEMENTS

It would be impossible to list all those to whom I am indebted for so much patience and help in gathering the information to write this book. They include, amongst others, Tenby boatmen and tradesmen, people who have lived and worked on Caldey over the years, and some who are still there, as well as those from further afield who have had business dealings with the Community. There are, too, ex-monks and ministers of religion of denominations other than Catholic. In asking all of these to accept a composite word of thanks I feel sure they will understand if I feel I must make a special individual mention of a small additional number.

Firstly, of course, there is Dom James Wicksteed, Abbot of Caldey, for his real help in the initial stages, when so much was a closed book to me, and especially for his kindness in so readily making the Abbey's Journal and other documents available to me and allowing me to quote from the Journal so copiously, as well as for allowing me to write this book at all.

On many occasions the members of the Community went to endless trouble in looking for old pictures and checking on details of which I was uncertain. Perhaps it was on Fr Stephen, the Procurator, that the brunt of this tedious burden fell. To Fr Anselm went the chief responsibility for ministering to my needs on the numerous occasions when I was privileged to be their guest. But it is to the Community as a whole that I must offer my thanks because the collective kindness, unassuming hospitality and genuine sense of friendship with which they unfailingly welcomed me must assuredly remain as an abiding memory long after other recollections have dimmed.

It is to an ex-monk of Caldey, Ron Howells (no relation), that I owe a particular debt of gratitude, because it was he who suggested I should write this book, and it was he who translated from the original French the extracts from the Monastery Journal. I have made reference in the script to the late Peter Anson's help, and Henry Kobus provided much valuable information concerning the perfume industry. I am also indebted to members of the staff in the National Library of Wales at Aberystwyth, the old Pembrokeshire County Library at Haverfordwest, Tenby Museum and the *Tenby Observer* office.

To all those who have helped, whether named herein or not, I am deeply grateful, for without their help, this book would not have been possible.

Finally, the work having been completed, I would like to express a special word of thanks to Dr Mervyn Stockwood, one of the more recent Caldey pilgrims, for so readily agreeing to write the Foreword.

R.H.

FOREWORD (1st Edition)

As a boy I was fascinated by Caldey Island. I vividly remember seeing a press photograph of the Benedictine monks leaving the Island for their new home at Prinknash. Many years later, it was during the war when I was a parson in Bristol, Dom Wilfred Upson, who had succeeded Aelred Carlyle as Abbot, invited me to spend some days at Prinknash to rest from the bombing. It was then that I met some of the foundation members who had started as Anglicans at Caldey before submitting to Rome. From them I learnt the early history and I became so interested that I promised myself that one day I would visit the Island. This promise was not fulfilled until 1970. Perhaps like good wine it was all the better for the delay in keeping. In any case it was a memorable experience—the beauty of the scenery, the inspiration of the services and the hospitality of the Abbot. I returned in 1975 and I hope I shall be allowed to make more pilgrimages in the years ahead.

It is a happy reflection that an Abbey which was once a cause of denominational bitterness is now a place to which Christians of many persuasions come. It has been my privilege to celebrate the Anglican Eucharist in the Abbot's Chapel and then to move to the Abbey church to join the Cistercian monks in their Mass.

The Cistercians are a contemplative order and talking is reduced to a minimum. Much of the day is spent in the chapel, but the monks do not escape worldly chores and responsibilities. Far from it. The Island has to be farmed and agricultural skills and hard manual work are required.

It is significant that this book about a Roman Catholic monastery should be written by a Free Churchman and this foreword by a Bishop of the Church of England. It bears witness to the fact that the peace and beauty of Caldey and the wide vision of the Abbot and his monks have proved to be a magnet. It is my hope that readers will find their interest so aroused that they will find their way to the Pembrokeshire coast and make a pilgrimage to this lovely place.

All Saints 1975   † MERVYN SOUTHWARK

NOTE TO THE THIRD EDITION

In the two decades since the first edition of this book, there have inevitably been many changes on Caldey, as there have been elsewhere. There have been deaths amongst the monastic Community, and there have been new arrivals. Some have tried their vocations and moved on, whilst others have stayed. At one time the numbers had fallen to as low as nine, but now they are up to twenty again. The Abbot, Dom James Wicksteed, having resigned after twenty-one years in that capacity, to undertake secular work, was succeeded by Dom Robert O'Brien.

All these things, however, have been recorded elsewhere, in *Caldey* with its much more detailed history of the Island, and *Farewell The Islands*. To keep everything up-to-date would almost call for an annual bulletin, which is not the purpose of this new edition.

This book was written originally to tell something of a monk's way of life, his beliefs and his objectives, of how the Cistercians came to Caldey, and something of the difficulties they had to face and overcome. In all these respects the work remains valid, and is being republished now in its original form because it is out-of-print and people continue to ask for it. To that there is neither need to add nor take away.

Man, so it is said, changes but little, God never. Just as the late J. C. Griffith Jones, as related in Chapter six, inveigled his way onto the island in the 1930's, masquerading as an archaeologist, to write a series of scurrilous articles for the *Western Mail*, so is there still the occasional similar deplorable happening. 'Twas ever thus. But against this must be set the infinitely greater number of journalists, radio and television producers, prepared to approach their task in a responsible manner and give their readers, listeners and viewers a proper appreciation of the life and work of the monastic Community.

Then there is the unique place which the Community has claimed in the affections, not only of the townspeople of Tenby, but of many much further afield, and the great work being done every year by the Friends of Caldey, an organisation now in its second decade and going from strength to strength.

The Friends come from all walks of life, and from other religious denominations as well as Catholics, but they have the one aim in common. That is, to enable the monastic Community to continue on the Island in their life of prayer. The Friends come to Caldey, by arrangement, for a period of a week or fortnight at a time, in groups of half-a-dozen or so, in order to do anything they can to help by way of painting, decorating, concreting, roofing, sawing up firewood, working in the gardens, or anything else to help.

For my own part I shall always consider myself to have been greatly privileged to have been allowed to write the book in the first place, and it has meant the forming of close and valued friendships. Eventually it led, as recorded in *Farewell The Islands*, to my doing the conducted tours of the monastery for six summer seasons. I recorded, too, how on one occasion I had replied to one irate questioner by saying, 'Now wait a minute. Don't misunderstand me. I'm not a Catholic. I'm a staunch Nonconformist.' I gave the same answer on a number of occasions. More recently the Abbot said to me, 'The trouble is, you've lost your punch line.'

From this it will be seen that I have not even sought to alter what is written in the Introduction to the first edition, where I said, 'I do not envisage myself as ever becoming any sort of convert, having found even the Anglican Church too high for me.'

As James Russell Lowell wrote, sometime in the last century, 'There is no good in arguing with the inevitable. The only argument available with an east wind is to put on your overcoat.'

Yes, I was received into the Catholic Church on October 29th, 1990, two days after my seventy-first birthday. And now I spend my time wondering why on earth I didn't get round to it years ago. My closeness to the monastic Community would undoubtedly have been the biggest single influence in my taking what must always be regarded as such an important step in anyone's life, so I never fail to tell them that on Judgement Day they may find they have more for which to answer than they think.

Still, it took Cardinal Newman a long time as well, and he was a much better man, and a much clearer thinker, than I could ever hope to be.

When I was received, my friends of the Abbey of Our Lady and St Samson on Caldey sent me two books, *The Cistercian Way*, by André Louf, and *Love Without Measure*, being extracts from the writings of St Bernard of Clairvaux, edited by Fr Paul Diemer, a Cistercian monk of Mount St Bernard. Both books had been signed by all the members of the Community, and they are, and will ever remain, treasured possessions.

It will be a treasured memory, too, that nearly all the members of what for so long had been my own Nonconformist chapel, as well as many representatives from other denominations in the area, were there when I was received. A step forward indeed, and a big step at that, on the road towards ecumenism.

These few explanations having been made at the outset, I am happy for the book, with a few minor corrections and amendments, to remain as it was when first published. At the same time, I would say a special thank you to Alan Shepherd for generously making available for the cover, pictures from his vast collection, which he has taken over the years for illustrating his own outstanding guide-books.

Finally, it means much to me that Bishop Mullins so readily agreed to write a Foreword to this new edition. For this, and for his friendship and encouragement ever since his appointment as Bishop of Minevia, I am truly grateful.

FOREWORD

When Catholic dioceses were re-established in England and Wales in 1850, none of the ancient names was used, with one exception. That one which was revived was the ancient title of Menevia, the Latin name for St. David's monastery and the name given to the territorial diocese that grew out of his evangelising mission in South West Wales.

In subsequent reorganisations of Catholic life in Wales, the Holy See has always retained the ancient title. In 1987, when a third diocese was created in Wales, the See of Menevia was restored to what is very nearly its ancient territorial boundaries.

Earlier in this century, monastic life was re-established on the venerable site on Caldey Island. The coming of the Cistercian monks brought back the Order that had been most significant in the life of Wales in medieval times. That they should come to a site that marked the earlier monastic tradition of this land was a new link in that long chain of Catholic Christianity which came to Wales with the Roman legions.

The erection of the present diocese of Menevia in 1987 was an act of faith. At a time when the Christian Faith was in decline in its ancient European strongholds, the Pope of Rome summoned the people of Menevia to build again on the foundations of St. David and St. Samson and all the saints of Wales.

To us here in Menevia, it is a matter of profound significance that one of the early signs of new life has been the revitalisation of the Cistercian community on Caldey. Like other forms of religious life, the monastery had been through difficult times. Only the power of the Holy Spirit at work in the Church can adequately explain the remarkable change that has taken place in a short time. The coming of the Cistercian sisters to the most venerable of all that Order's sites, at Whitland, is surely a promise that the grace of God is again at work in this land of Wales and in this Church of Menevia.

The monastery on Caldey has had a special apostolate in Wales. Centuries of division and of misunderstanding had created suspicion and mistrust among Christians. By being true to the vision and to the rule of the founders of the Order, the monks on Caldey have been a focus of unity and of developing harmony for all of us. Without deviating from the strict observance of their way of life, the Community have provided a welcome and an inspiration for all who seek to follow Christ. Clergy of many Churches have found there a haven of prayer; there we have all learned to pray.

In former times, the Cistercian Order had a special place in the affection of Welsh people. The monasteries became centres of Welsh culture. Young men from all backgrounds formed the communities. The history and the literature of Wales was recorded and preserved in the monastic libraries. The life of the Welsh nation was supported and made holy by the prayers of the monks.

It will be so again when young men from Wales begin to join the community on Caldey. For that has been a gap in the history of the monastery in this century. With the re-issue of *Total Community* and its wide dissemination in our parishes, it is my confident hope that this will be an important part of the rebuilding of the Diocese of Menevia. I look forward to the day when many of the novices and monks on Caldey will be from the homes and families of Wales.

† DANIEL J. MULLINS
Bishop of Menevia

ILLUSTRATIONS

Between pages 40/41

The founding monks leaving Chimay in Belgian, December, 1928

Passing through Cardiff on the way to Caldey

The 'Founding Fathers' on Caldey, January 6th, 1929. In the centre, Dom Anselm le Bail

A Visit by Dr Vaughan, Bishop of Menevia, April 1929

The first Novitiates, June 5th, 1929: Above, before, and below, after their reception

A trip to the mainland, 1929

Andre Garcette (left). The first Cistercian Prior of Caldey, together with Fr Ivor Daniel, then Priest at Pembroke Dock

Removal of the bells from Caldey to Prinknash, May 31st, 1931

The Old Priory as it was in the 1930's

The *Stephen Harding*, one of the early Island boats, 1933

Taking coal from the beached coal boat to the Island store. *c.* 1930

An early haymaking scene. *c.* 1930

Brother Teilo fishing in the Old Priory fishpond. 1931

The Community photographed on January 14th, 1934

Reaping and binding in July 1934

The Island generator. *c.* 1933

The High Altar (later burnt) showing the Pre-Reformation stones sent from other monasteries

At work on the Island. *c.* 1935

Unloading coal from the beach. *c.* 1938

Tenby boatmen reading the Prior's notice restricting landing on Sundays and out of 'Season', August 24th, 1936

Timber washed up at Sandtop bay, November 26th, 1938

The first six monks to be called up on the outbreak of war, September 1939

The Norwegian ship *Belpareil* aground at Little Drinkim bay, January 1940

A visit from officers of the Belgian Army, August 1940

Between pages 104/105

The 'Cottage' Monastery and Church: above, before and below, after the fire of September 25th, 1940

The Tenby firemen and volunteers who fought the fire on Caldey

The burnt-out Church

Taking pigs to the mainland in the *Crimson Rambler*, April 1941

The wreck of the *Crimson Rambler* at Eel Point, October 1941

An amphibious craft on Caldey during the D Day rehearsals off the Pembroke-shire coast

The burial, without a coffin, of Dom Aelred le Fevre, March 1st, 1942

Dom Albert Derzelle, Prior of Caldey, 1946 to 1954

The temporary Church as it was in 1949

FOR A GOLDEN JUBILEE

Fifty years in God's service,
  This is for me real bliss!
Souvenirs of warm union,
  Memories of great pardon,
Days of desolation—
  Hours of consolation.

Praise and Thanksgiving
  Be to Christ our King!
Fifty years of seeking
  The Invisible Being.
Five decades of longing
  To enjoy God's blessings;
Five decades of trusting
  In Him for everything.

Praise and Thanksgiving
  Be to Christ our King!
Each year starting anew
  Helped by heavenly dew:
Each day fighting afresh
  The devil and the flesh.
With hardly lull or rest
  An every day contest.

Praise and Thanksgiving
  Be to Christ our King!
The full day shall dawn,
  As the morrow must come.
Although dusk it is still—
  The sun behind the hill—
The dawn of Eternity
  Is now my Felicity!

Praise and Thanksgiving
  Be to Christ our King!
O God, three in One. . .
  Delay not, do come!

Fr Pascal, Caldey (died 1979)

INTRODUCTION

Most people are fascinated by islands, whilst monks, living a life so out of tempo with the frighteningly increasing speed of our present day civilisation, also tend to cause a measure of interest and speculation. Take the two together and we have sufficient to create the sort of interest inevitably aroused by something different, especially when, as in the case of Caldey, the focal point is so close to, and indeed in view of, thousands of town-dwelling holidaymakers who throng the South Pembrokeshire coast throughout the summer season. Immediately, there is a sense of mystery and it whets the appetite of the curious.

There are others, very many in number, who know Caldey well and go there whenever they can because, long ago, they were captivated by its charm and came under the spell of its atmosphere of peace and tranquillity. Some there are, too, who go there because of their need for spiritual revival and refreshment.

It may be said, and with a considerable degree of truth, that I am ill-qualified to attempt to write in any great detail on such a subject. I accept the validity of any such assertion but, in all humility, am prepared to state what I believe to be moderate qualifications for at least making the attempt.

I was brought up in South Pembrokeshire and have lived most of my life with the Island in full view across the bay. I was a boy in an age when the the proper thing in a predominantly Nonconformist area was to dislike Roman Catholics and be suspicious of them. If I have lived to see the folly of such an attitude, and to decide for myself that the world today leaves no room for such differences, I cannot think that I am in any peril because of it. At least, any sympathy I may be accused of having towards the monks cannot be directly attributed to anything other than such personal assessments as I have been able to make for myself.

Certainly I would make no pretence to knowing a great deal about the Roman Catholic faith. Still less could I claim to be an authority on monasticism. I do not envisage myself as ever becoming any sort of convert, having found even the Anglican Church too high for me. But then, a man who finds God in a wood, or any other lonely place, may think it odd that I should get anything out of going to Chapel. It does not mean that either of us is right or wrong, but it does mean, I hope, that I have fundamental beliefs strong enough to know that what is right for the other man is where he finds the most spiritual comfort.

Then there is the temporal aspect of the monks' existence. By long tradition they are of agricultural pursuit. I suppose I can say I know something about farming. Rather more important, I have had occasion to study, more than many, the history of those people who have struggled for a living by farming Pembrokeshire's islands and am therefore not unfamiliar with the problems that are involved.

I must also confess to being one who loves the peace of Caldey and its unique atmosphere. In addition, I can claim a more personal interest because my grandmother, when she married in 1875, made her first home on Caldey, where my grandfather was employed as a gardener. Their first child, my mother's sister, was born and christened there.

Over the years I have come to know some of the monks. If their attitude and bearing have led me to think that the Roman faith was not quite as bad as I had been brought up to believe, I am not prepared to accept that I have been dangerously influenced by the insidious propaganda of a great evil hidden beneath a charming exterior. It could just be that they are better ambassadors for Christ than so many of their detractors.

These pages, then, will be concerned almost exclusively with the Cistercian monks of Caldey and their life there since 1929. Much has been written of Caldey in other times. There is no point in repeating a great deal of it here. There are gaps which could be filled by writing at some length of those who struggled for a living on the Island over the years before this century. But their story would no doubt be similar in many ways to that of people who struggled for a living on other islands, except that on Caldey there has always been a community and, at times, a quarrying industry, besides the traditional farming.

No serious attempt, however, has ever been made to tell the story of the present monastic Community, on the only Pembrokeshire island now being farmed. My abiding hope is that when that story has been told I shall be as welcome there as I have always been for more years than I care to remember.

1
CALDEY'S MONASTIC HISTORY

*'Your old men shall dream dreams,
and your young men shall see visions.'*: Joel 2:28

Situated off the south coast of Pembrokeshire, three miles by boat from Tenby harbour, Caldey extends to something like five hundred and sixty acres, and considerably more than half of this area is now being farmed.

The climate is equable but the prevailing wind from the south-west, laden with salt from the Atlantic, sweeps the Island so that, in the exposed parts, there are no trees or hedgegrowth. The field boundaries therefore are mostly of stone-walling. Where the Island slopes away from the west and south, trees and shrubs thrive. The whole place is a paradise for botanists, and it has great attractions for ornithologists, too, even though, mainly because of the presence of rats, the seabirds are not as numerous as on the other Pembrokeshire islands. In the autumn, the grey Atlantic seals come to the Island's lonely caves and beaches to give birth to their young.

Recently excavated human remains and flint instruments of the Stone Age, as well as the bones of animals long-extinct in Britain, establish that the history of the Island goes back to at least 10,000 B.C., before which date Caldey was still attached to the mainland.

The name, Caldey, was given to it much later by the Norsemen and means Cold Island and not, as some would have it to be, Island of the Spring. The earlier Welsh name was Ynys Pyr, either after Pyr y Dwyrain, from whom Manorbier Castle takes its name, or after Pyro, its first Abbot, way back in the sixth century. Pyro had retired to Caldey as a hermit, and a small community grew up there living, according to the Celtic custom, in wattle huts grouped round the chapel. When he died he was succeeded as Abbot by Samson, who had come to Caldey from St Illtyd's Abbey at Llantwit Major in Glamorgan. Samson later sailed to Brittany to become the first Bishop of Dol where he founded a monastery.

This Community of Celtic monks on Caldey might have been slaughtered by the Norsemen who raided the coast in the tenth century, but no evidence has ever been discovered to confirm this or, indeed, to suggest their presence or occupation of the Island at any time. In the twelfth century, however, the Island saw a return to the monastic way of life, for in 1131 Henry I gave Caldey to a Norman nobleman, Robert Fitz Martin. Fitz Martin gave it to his mother and she, in turn, gave it to the monks of St Dogmael's, a Benedictine house from the Abbey of Tiron in France, who had established their monastery in North Pembrokeshire. Caldey thus became a Priory of St Dogmael's and continued so until the suppression by Henry VIII in 1536. The remains of the 14th century buildings have been incorporated in what has now become known as the Old Priory. Little is known of their history but, when the monks had been expelled, the Island was granted to a John Bradshaw of Presteigne, and this will be found to have considerable significance in the period with which we shall be chiefly dealing.

It was almost four centuries before monasticism again returned to Caldey. The Island had been bought in 1897 by the Rev Done Bushell, a master and chaplain at Harrow School, who had a mentally handicapped son for whom the Island could provide a measure of privacy. Done Bushell spent a great deal of capital and did much hard work in restoring some of the old buildings, notably the Old Priory and the two churches of St Illtyd's and St David's. Two years later he invited Benjamin Fearnley Carlyle, who had assumed the name of Dom Aelred, to bring his half-dozen Anglican Benedictine monks to establish a monastery on Caldey, and he sold the Island to them in 1906 after the death of his son. This Community was received into the Roman Catholic Church in 1913. Carlyle resigned and went to Canada in 1921.

Those are the bare facts and sufficient for the guide book. Here, however, more consideration is necessary, because Carlyle's sojourn on the Island was the reason for the eventual arrival of the Cistercians, and the monastery he built remains, not only as a commanding feature of the Island, but as a monument to his megalomania and self-delusion. He heaped insupportable financial burdens upon his followers, and led them into such difficulty that only the intervention of the Cistercians saved them from bankruptcy.

The hopeless situation created by Carlyle at once provided the need and the justification for the coming of the present Order to Caldey. Whether the move proves to have been to the ultimate good of the Cistercian Order will be for history to judge, but it is probably true, and only fair, to say that, without the foundations laid before their coming, their remarkable achievements to date would hardly have been possible. Almost thirty years earlier, in 1901, when religious Orders were being expelled from France, Cistercian monks visited Caldey to ascertain whether it would be possible to establish a foundation on the Island in the event of the Rev Done Bushell being prepared to sell it. They decided that the Island would be too small for practical agriculture and acquired properties instead at Woodbarton, in South Devon, and at Martin, near Salisbury, but returned eventually to France. Their decision concerning the size of the Island will be worth remembering in a later chapter.

The complete story of Carlyle's life has been told in comprehensive detail by Peter Anson in his remarkable book, *Abbot Extraordinary* (1958), and there are further references to the Caldey part of his life in the same author's books, *Benedictines of Caldey* (1940), and *Building Up The Waste Places* (1973). The book, *Abbot Extraordinary*, however, being about Carlyle, gives a marvellous first-hand account, often told with great humour, of what went on.

At various periods from 1910 to 1924, Peter Anson was a member of the Community which Dom Aelred had founded on Caldey and he remained a close friend of this restless visionary until the latter's death in 1955. Peter Anson left the Order in 1924 but, in 1969, at the age of eighty, he was invited by the present Community to come 'home' to Caldey to spend his remaining years. Recognised as a world authority on monastic history, he nevertheless came in for a measure of criticism for writing as frankly as he did about a life-long friend. He died at the age of eighty-six on July 10th, 1975.

To give the book its due, it is unquestionably a most valuable contribution to the history of Caldey. Perhaps those who criticise do so because to the pure all things are pure. If the author referred to Carlyle's weaknesses, he also paid ample tribute to his many good qualities, and he remained his friend in spite of his faults. He could have argued perhaps that the duty of a friend is to excuse faults and accept them, rather than pretend they never existed, and that he did not say all that he could have said. As a result of some of Carlyle's actions, half-a-dozen professed monks left the Island, some to join other Benedictine Communities, and one wrote a letter of complaint to the Roman authorities. Following the Apostolic Visitation by three special visitors appointed by the Holy See, which took place in 1921, Carlyle left quietly, quickly, and under a considerable cloud, for British Columbia.

When I was discussing this controversy with Peter Anson he said, 'Whatever conclusions you draw or whatever you write, mind, remember that Carlyle was a most lovable man.' With a beautiful voice and compelling eyes he seems to have had an almost hypnotic influence on some of those with whom he came into contact. He was one of the rare people able to handle Done Bushell's handicapped, and sometimes violent, son, and the goodwill engendered by this was partially why the Rev Bushell did so much for Carlyle. By means of a pen that could hardly ever have been still, and with a tongue of silver, Carlyle charmed many and varied benefactors to part with large sums of money to further his grandiose schemes.

To look at the Abbey as it is today the visitor could be forgiven for thinking that this was his great dream come true. Nothing could be further from the truth. To Carlyle it was just a modest beginning. The real vision, for which plans were drawn in 1906 and again in 1917, was of an immense Abbey which was to be built on the cliff-top above Paul Jones' Bay at the east of the Island. The present Abbey, built between 1910 and 1913, was intended to serve eventually merely as a preparatory school. It contained magnificent quarters for the Abbot, quite out of keeping with any ideas of monastic austerity. With a high tower, from the top of which Dom Aelred could see all over the Island, the white-washed red-roofed building contained all sorts of odd gables and minarets. The ideas for these useless appendages were no doubt prompted in some measure by his sporadic visits to the Continent, and they resulted in an edifice which, whilst being somewhat mediaeval in appearance, is also a typical and fitting reminder of its eccentric creator.

The same influence can be seen in other buildings on the Island, amongst them the present post office with its odd-shaped roof. A chapel was added to the row of cottages in which the monks lived before the new building was completed and, for the altar of this chapel, stones were brought from the ruins of old monasteries all over England.

Even after the money that was begged from people was taken into account, the vast building programme undertaken was hopelessly beyond the meagre income which the Community were able to earn. Probably at no time were they able even to support themselves.

However grandiose Carlyle's schemes may have been, and to whatever extent they may or may not have been the result of personal ambition, when he paid a visit to Caldey in 1951 at the age of seventy-seven, he was thrilled and gratified to see that the stability of which he had dreamed was being brought to fruition by the Cistercians, and he wrote in glowing and excited terms of the way in which they were living and conducting their affairs.

Following his ignominious departure in 1921, the remainder of the Community struggled on bravely, but more than £20,000 in debt. Whilst the future of their Community was still under discussion, there came rumours that the Church of England would be prepared to buy the Island, a prospect entirely unacceptable at that time to the Catholics. Pope Pius XI appealed to the Reformed Cistercian Order in 1924 to purchase the property and, although in 1925 this was done, it was hard to see how this could benefit the Community. Two French monks from Thymadeuc were installed as bailiffs and took charge of the Island accounts, with the Benedictines as their tenants. During these years Mr Thomas Dyer-Edwardes offered them a new house at Prinknash, near Gloucester, where they moved in the autumn of 1928 to found a house which has continued to flourish. Foundations were made at Farnborough, in Hampshire, in 1927, and at Pluscarden, in Moray, the following year. Previously to that, when Caldey went over to Rome in 1913, two internal oblates of the Community, retaining their Anglican allegiance, founded an

Anglican Community of Benedictines at Pershore in Worcester. In 1926 they moved to Nashdom, in Berkshire, where they celebrated their jubilee in 1964, having raised a foundation at St Gregory's, Three Rivers, Michigan, in 1939.

This, then, is something of the monastic history of Caldey and its buildings. Here, too, are some of the problems which the Cistercian monks were inheriting when they moved into their Island home in January 1929.

2
CISTERCIAN HISTORY

'The wilderness and the solitary place shall be glad for them; and the desert shall rejoice, and blossom as the rose': Isiah 35:1

At the same time as the early Celtic monks were on Caldey, monasticism was flourishing and spreading on the Continent. One stream reached Italy very soon after its beginning in Egypt and Palestine, and it was there, in Italy, that St Benedict, early in the sixth century, wrote his Rule for the monastic life, basing it on the Gospels and the experience of his monastic predecessors. A wise and balanced Rule, its first aim was not austerity, but the love of God and all mankind, with the monk's daily life envisaged as a sensible mixture of prayer, manual work and studious, spiritual reading.

Eventually, and no doubt inevitably, problems arose. A love of wealth began to creep in. Persecution, invasion and plague all made their impact and brought many lapses and reforms, so that many changes had been made to the Rule itself by the time of William the Conqueror.

In 1098, a group of monks in the monastery of Molesme, led by their Abbot, St Robert, left the Abbey there and settled in the wilderness of Citeaux, near Dijon in Burgundy, where they founded a new Order. It took its name from the Latin name for Citeaux, which was Cistercium.

The Cistercians set themselves as far as possible to return to the simple life envisaged in the Rule of St Benedict, choosing 'to be poor with the poor Christ.' Amongst the reeds of the surrounding marshlands, they dug wells, felled trees and built a wooden church and huts. They lived on a simple diet of vegetables and wore the cheapest cloth. One particular result of their return to the original Rule was an insistence that they should live by the work of their own hands, with the consequent rejection of the practice of accepting as endowments either tithes or manors which they could not work themselves. This practice, they knew, was one of the things which had contributed to declining standards in the Benedictine Order.

The following year St Robert was recalled to Molesme and he was succeeded as Abbot of Citeaux by St Alberic, who, amongst other things, introduced Lay Brothers to the Order. These members of the Community took their vows but did not have the same rights or duties as their fellows. There was a distinction then between manual and menial labour, but it is a distinction which has now become a thing of the past. A year later St Alberic was followed as Abbot by an Englishman, St Stephen Harding. He continued with the reformed regime but safeguarded the Rule with new legislation.

For the first eleven years no new arrivals came, men saying the life was impossible, whilst sickness took its toll of the monks. St Stephen Harding, however, held firm and, in the end, emerged triumphant. He gave the Cistercians their 'Charter of Charity' which ensured that the same pattern of life would be lived in every monastery founded within the new Order. Today, not only does the Abbot of every Mother House visit his daughter Abbeys, which is known as the Annual Visitation, but every Abbot is also expected to go to Rome every three years to the General Chapter and thus draw from its very source the spirit of the Order. All this in order that the same spirit of Christ should everywhwere and at all times prevail.

Great and firm though the foundations were for which these founding Abbots had been responsible, the turning point came, when future prospects looked bleak indeed, with the arrival in 1112, of St Bernard and thirty of his friends and relations whom he had persuaded to join him. This young nobleman, courteous and charming, had as his one ambition, the desire to imitate the life of Christ in obscurity in this new, almost unknown monastery, lost to the world. Man proposes, however, but God disposes. Three years after his arrival at Citeaux, St Bernard became Abbot of Clairvaux, the fourth Abbey of the new Order. He became one of the great figures of the Middle Ages, leaving behind some marvellous writing which has endured through the ages, full of humanity and an intense search for God. By the time he died in 1153 his own Abbey of Clairvaux alone had founded sixty-eight new monasteries. Two of them were in Wales.

The first Cistercians to come to Wales were the monks of

Tintern, who arrived in 1131, and they became a flourishing Community. It was the beginning of the 'Golden Age' for monasteries, which was to last for more than two hundred years. The Cistercian life during this period was one of secluded communal intercession and worship. The monasteries were always built in remote situations, with the churches, and the vestments worn being plain in character, and the members of the Community maintaining their strict Rule on diet and silence. Monastic manual labour was given its primitive prominent position and in every country the Cistercians became important agricultural pioneers.

The system they developed for working their outlying land was to make full use of lay brothers, as introduced to the Order by St Alberic. The monks themselves, with their church services seven times a day, were not usually able to work very far from the monastery. The lay brothers had not the same obligation to sing the church offices as the monks and were able to spend more time working. For the most part they were unlettered men. Round the monastery, wherever they had land, the monks would build granges where a group of lay brothers could work and eat and sleep during the week, returning to the monastery on Sundays and the great feast days.

Occasionally, of course, the arrangement led to problems. At the General Chapter at Citeaux in 1195 the following decree was made: 'The Abbots of Wales are commanded that in their granges no beer is to be drunk, nor any drink but plain water.' One of the reasons for this decree is to be found in another decree of the same General Chapter: 'The Lay Brothers of Wales who took away the horses of the Abbot of Cwmhir because he forbade them beer are to come to Clairvaux on foot and stand to the judgement of the Abbot of Clairvaux.' It was a long walk indeed and, in view of the evident predilections of the Brothers involved, it is tempting, and perhaps permissible, to wonder whether it developed into the longest pub crawl in history.

In spite of these occasional troubles, however, monks and lay brothers did get through a great deal of serious work. When the first Cistercians arrived, there must still have been a considerable area of land in Wales which had never been cultivated and it was this which usually formed the endowments of their monasteries. It meant that before they could grow wheat they had to clear away the oak trees, but timber was too useful a commodity for them to do that with all their land.

In 1140 the first Cistercians settled in Pembrokeshire at Little Treffgarne, five miles north of Haverfordwest. In 1151 this Community moved to Whitland. Later, Whitland established two foundations in Ireland, having already made previous foundations at Cwm-hir in Radnorshire, Strata Florida in Cardiganshire, Strata Marcella near Welshpool, Cymer near Dolgellau, Llantarnam in Monmouthshire, Aberconwy (originally where the town of Conwy now stands, but later moved further up the river to make way for a royal castle), and Valley Crucis near Llangollen. Strata Florida was the most prominent because of its long association with the Welsh princes.

In all these places the same pattern of life went on with the same daily, weekly and yearly round of work on the land. Little by little monks and lay brothers advanced, clearing a little more land, growing a little more corn, shearing a few more sheep year after year, each generation trying to leave the land that much better than they found it, each generation trying to find new ways of coping with an ever-changing situation. Even then, indeed, each generation 'living as though they would die today and farming as though they would live forever', just as good farmers have done throughout the ages.

By the middle of the fourteenth century the picture had begun to change. In many monasteries discipline had started to become lax and a steady decline set in, due to increasing wealth and the gradual disappearance of the lay brothers. 'To be poor with the poor Christ' had been the spirit to keep the Order dependent on God and therefore close to Him. That union, however, began to weaken when the Order's own manual labour began to make monks wealthy.

Wars and the Black Death then took their toll, to be followed by the Reformation in the sixteenth century with its suppression of the monasteries in Britain. Most of them fell into ruins. But later, and by way of a reaction against the decline, a new Congregation, that of the Strict Observance, sprang up on the Continent, the best known centre of which was that of La

Trappe, founded in 1664. For a time, unremitting penance took the place of St Benedict's balance and moderation. Perhaps, in present day jargon, it would be said that they 'over-reacted', for their reforming austerity went far beyond anything laid down in the Rule.

Early in the seventeenth century the Order began to be divided into Communities which followed the Common Observance, to distinguish them from those who adopted the Strict Observance. The latter developed rapidly after Armand de Rancé became regular Abbot of La Trappe.

In the late eighteenth century the French Revolution swept the monasteries and convents away, and for three years as many as two hundred and forty monks and nuns wandered homeless through Europe and Russia, but even in the depths of winter remaining faithful to the Rule. In the 1790's Cistercian monastic life was resumed in Britain when some of the monks exiled from France founded a Community at Lulworth in Dorset, but after the fall of Napoleon they returned to France. The name of this Community is still coupled with that of the Cistercians of the Strict Observance because they were the only group of these monks to survive the French Revolution. This fact creates the link between St Robert of 1098 and modern Citeaux.

In 1892 Pope Leo XIII divided the Order into two distinct branches, Cistercians of the Common Observance, and Cistercians of the More Strict Observance, sometimes known as Reformed Cistercians. It is still common for people to refer to the Reformed Cistercians as Trappists, but this is not strictly correct. When the Reformed Cistercian Order was created in 1892 most of the houses still followed the rigid Constitutions drawn up for the Abbey of La Trappe in 1664. But *new* Constitutions, based on the primitive usages of Citeaux, were approved in 1894, confirmed in 1902, and revised in 1925.

The monastery near Chimay, in the Belgian province of Hainault, was founded in 1850 by successors of the monks of La Trappe. The idea came from the Abbé Jourdain, curé of Virelles, who approached the Abbot of Westmalle, near Antwerp, which had been revived in 1814 after the French Revolution, and eventually the Prince de Chimay gave lands under certain conditions. The Abbé of St Sixtus, near Poperinghe, which had itself been revived from Westmalle in 1831, agreed to provide pioneers. When they arrived on July 22nd, 1850, they found a lonely, exposed site where the soil was rocky and the climate damp. It was the start of what was to become the Abbey of Notre Dame de Scourmont.

The handful of monks, with no money and facing great difficulties, lived in an old farmhouse and sheds. Very slowly, conditions improved and by stages a large monastery and a church were built. In 1871 Notre Dame de Scourmont became an Abbey, with Dom Hyacinthe Bouteca, one of the St Sixtus pioneer monks, becoming the first Abbot. In addition to farming, a brewery was established to become the chief source of income.

By 1928 the Breton, Dom Anselme le Bail, was the Abbot and there were eighty monks at Chimay. This was the house from which the founding pioneers came to Caldey, an island of infinite charm, but situated in what was to them a foreign land.

3
FOUNDATION ON CALDEY

*'Wait on the Lord: be of good courage, and He shall strengthen
thine heart'*: Psalm 27:14

Having taken this brief look at the monastic history of Caldey,
and given some consideration to the centuries-old story of the
Cistercians themselves, we must now look in more detail at the
decision of the Chimay monks to establish a settlement on
Caldey, the events which led up to it, and something of the
problems that were involved in the move. There can hardly be
a better way than to quote freely, and almost in its entirety,
from the account in the Records of Caldey Abbey written by
hand in French. It is an account which has never previously
been published, and was in fact only discovered in the course
of research for this work. Although very brief mention has been
made in passing of some of the events referred to, there is no
harm in further reference to them again. The fact that they
have already been mentioned will make for a more ready
understanding in the context of this extract from a unique
chronicle. In quoting from the records, certain passages have
been printed exactly as they were written over forty years ago,
but other sections have been rewritten to form a thread of
continuity linking the extracts.

The Records of Caldey Abbey

On March 21st,1928, feast of St Benedict, after a novena of
prayers and study, the Chapter of the Abbey of Notre Dame de
Scourmont voted and accepted the principle to establish the
foundation on Caldey Island (Great Britain).

April 9th, 1928. After a brief explanation of the conditions by the
Rev Abbot General of the Cistercian Order, the same Chapter
voted and decided definitely to accept the foundation.

It was 1.30 p.m. March 14th, 1928, in the study room at
Scourmont, that the Community had assembled to be told of the
project of founding a monastery on Caldey Island.

The meeting began with prayers to the Holy Spirit for guidance, and a request for the intercession of St Benedict, St Stephen Harding, St Aelred and all the Saints of Caldey.

Agenda:—
1. History of the question.
2. Reasons for foundation.
3. Monastic recruitment.
4. Places for a foundation.
5. Conditions for a foundation.

1. *History*

For five years the Abbey of Notre Dame de Scourmont (Chimay —Belgium) had been considering the necessity of founding a daughter house. The Reverend Father Abbot had examined possibilities in many countries, including Japan, Congo, India, Madagascar, Switzerland, Poland and Spain.

In order to advance his plan, the Abbot approached the Reverend Abbot General at the General Chapter of 1927 and offered to accept any request for a foundation that was available. In February, 1928, the Abbot General invited the Abbot of Scourmont to accompany him to England, and they spent a week on Caldey Island where there was already a Benedictine Monastery (of Anglican converts). The Community, however, were probably leaving the Island very soon—and a foundation would be possible. No decision was made then.

2. *Reason for foundation at Caldey on our part*

(a) The Community at Scourmont was at this time increasing rapidly, many good novices were presenting themselves, and the ranks of the solemnly professed monks continued to multiply. There was developing a serious situation of accommodation.

(b) There was at that time a feeling for the need of a daughter house, that if necessary could act as another home in the event of persecution or expulsion. England was considered very tolerant, and into the bargain there was at Caldey a monastery already constructed.

3. *Reasons for foundation on part of the Church and the Cistercian Order*

The Catholic Church was most anxious that this monastic Island should continue to be occupied by monks and the Cistercian Order in particular.

(a) *History of the Benedictine Community of Caldey*

The Community of Anglican Benedictines led by Dom Aelred Carlyle had bought the Island in 1906. These Anglican monks followed a Rule very little different from that of the Cistercians, the basis of their lives being the Divine Office, study and manual work, and this remained so until 1913. In this year most of the Community were received into the Catholic Church and, as a result, they lost the support and financial assistance of their patrons in the Anglican Church. Very soon they were unable to pay their way and, in spite of a journey by Dom Aelred to U.S.A. to seek help, they were in fact facing bankruptcy.

It was thus that Rome, being anxious to keep this Island, so full of monastic history, requested the Cistercian Order to purchase it. The Abbot General agreed, and the Island, all its buildings, its materials and its livestock, passed to the Cistercians of the Strict Observance. This took place in 1925 and it was agreed that the Benedictine Community should remain there for three years in order to try finally to establish themselves, and if successful, to purchase. The three years expired in December, 1928, and the Benedictine monks of Caldey were still unable to seek re-possession.

(b) *Offer to our Community*
So it came about that, after much searching within the Order, the Cistercians of Notre Dame de Scourmont, Chimay in Belgium, decided to accept the responsibility of Caldey Island.

(c) *Possibility of the Cistercian life in England is a question that had to be asked and examined*
Firstly on our part, and secondly on the part of the country receiving us.

Notre Dame de Scourmont could send at least ten choir monks as founders, more later if necessary—and about three lay brothers, depending on the need. There was in fact personnel available.

We were receiving plenty of signs that we would be welcomed by the Church in England—and that our future could be said to be hopeful. Our monastic predecessors had no shortage of vocations in following a Rule very similar to our own. Mount St Bernard—the only other Cistercian monastery in Great Britain—had at this time (1928) eleven novices, whilst the Cistercian nuns at Stapehill (Dorset) were thinking of founding a House themselves because of their great numbers.

Caldey itself in addition had a long history of monastic life, including Celtic monks of the fifth century, and Benedictines from the twelfth to the sixteenth. The English people are aware of this and we may certainly hope they want very much to keep it so.

We have the encouragement and protection of Cardinal Bourne, Archbishop of Westminster, who has obtained permission for us to

enter and settle in Great Britain. In addition, Bishop Vaughan of
Menevia and Ordinary of Caldey is very favourably disposed
towards our monks, and finally our own Rev Fr Abbot General has
great confidence in the future.

(d) *Material position*
   Site. The entire island will be placed at the disposal of the
Cistercian monks, there to take up their abode without restriction
(except, of course, the lighthouse).
   Monastery. This contains church, chapter house, refectory, study
rooms, kitchen, bakery, workshops, cloisters, dormitories etc.
   Development of the land. While the island is of 240 hectares it
appears that much remains uncultivated and the possibility of a
great increase in this direction must be considered. The soil is good
and we may expect to develop the production of vegetables. And
something that may be the envy of those left in the Mother House
at Chimay—peaches, figs and vines in the greenhouses of Caldey!
Water is available for drinking and all domestic purposes.
   The farm is about 300 metres from the monastery. It contains
sheds for 100 cows, a barn and threshing machine. In brief, all the
complete material of an English farm, but the condition leaves
much to be desired.
   Livestock: 8 good horses, 50 cows (milking), 110 sheep, 15 lambs
over one year, 11 under one year, 300 Leghorn chickens (which
could, in view of accommodation, be increased to 800), and finally
we list our brother Donkey.
   Workshops: As laid down in the Rule of St Benedict, the monastery
contains all the workshops necessary for the needs of the
Community, together with generator and batteries for the supply
of electricity.
   Boat: For the daily trips between the Island and the mainland the
monastery possesses a motorboat of 30 h.p.
   Guesthouse etc: There are two guesthouses available for the
monastery and many houses on the Island. Most of the latter are
let and each brings in a rent of £25 p.a.

   On Saturday March 17th, 1928, the Chapter of the Community
of Notre Dame de Scourmont met again to consider the
question of the foundation of Caldey.
   The problems were pointed out. Sacrifices would have to be
made. The hours of manual work could be long, and many
difficulties could arise. The date of the departure of the
Benedictines from Caldey had not been fixed, but their leaving

the Island now seemed certain. Caldey Island was now available to any monastery of the Order of Citeaux. Chimay, however, did not seem to have any competition, and it merely remained for the approval of the General Chapter. It would be necessary to send two religious to Caldey in order to study the situation, and especially with regard to the necessity for earning a living from the Island.

A further meeting was held on March 21st, 1928, and as a result it was agreed that 'Our House, in consideration of our numbers, found a Community and arrange for the definite departure of thirteen members of the Community (ten choir monks and three lay brothers).'

On the same day the Abbot of Notre Dame de Scourmont, Dom Anselm le Bail, notified the Rev Fr Abbot General of the result of the vote of the Conventual Chapter. On March 27th he invited the Abbot General to come to Chimay and address the Community.

On Easter Sunday of that year the Abbot General, in the Chapter of the monastery, explained to the assembled Community and novices the conditions necessary for the foundation of Caldey. Thus Caldey became the responsibility of the Cistercian monks of Chimay in Belgium.

On June 24th, 1928, (at the Chapter of Chimay) Dom Anselm announced the names of the three monks to form an advance party. They were Fr Andrew Garcette (Sub-Prior of Chimay), Fr Basil Ragon and Br Alberic.

After a holiday with their families they left for Caldey on July 10th, accompanied by Dom Anselm. In London they were received by His Eminence Cardinal Bourne and Mgr Cardon de Wiart. They were received at Caldey by the Benedictines who, of course, were still on the Island. The advance party concerned themselves with studying the material conditions and the administration, and familiarising themselves with the English language and customs. Dom Anselm was accompanied on his return to Belgium by two monks of Notre Dame de Thymadeuc, Cistercians who had been concerned with the administration of the Island following the purchase by the Order in 1925.

In September of this year (1928) the foundation was confirmed when news was received that the Benedictines were finally and definitely unable to remain on the Island. On the 27th of that month Fr Basil returned to Chimay to make preparations for the movement of the founder members.

At the beginning of November Dom Anselm decided to send three more religious to Caldey, and on the fourteenth Fr Rémy, Br Barthelemy and Br Andrew left to assist as the Benedictines prepared to leave. They were accompanied by Fr Andrew Garcette, and spent a day in London visiting St Paul's, Westminster Cathedral, Westminster Abbey and the Houses of Parliament in the company of a Lord. Proceeding to Tenby on the sixteenth they found a very heavy sea and were obliged to spend the night in the town. They crossed the next day, but between the rain and the wind their first impression was painful and disagreeable. The six of the advance party slept at the Old Priory, and said Mass there, but spent the rest of the day working and sharing the common life of the Benedictines.'

From the Caldey Island Journal we read,

'Dec 3rd. Br Andrew took over the milking operation. About tis time, which shows the mildness of the climate, there were still potatoes in the ground. It was decided to gather them, but what a sad harvest—20 kilo in a row of 300 metres!

Dec 20th. At 9 a.m. this morning the last party of the Benedictines finally left the Island, and Fr Andrew Garcette left for Chimay to make the final preparations for the move.

Christmas Day, 1928. Mass at midnight was said by Fr Rémy, while the villagers provided the singing. After the Mass they (the villagers) were received in the guest-house for a light supper (*reveillon*) and they were all delighted with the reception. Fr Basil sang the High Mass the next morning. After Vespers and Benediction, a custom very dear to the English, that of singing Christmas carols, was performed.

During this time much activity had been going on at Chimay in preparation for what was to be a big operation. Each monk's complete outfit, including a clergyman's suit, complete set of vestments, collection of choir books, certain items of furniture, some books to found a library etc. etc. had to be prepared. Fr Bertin, Fr Dominic and Br Christopher were in charge of packing. The mode of transport would be a wagon direct from Forges-lez-Chimay to Tenby, and on Dec 24th the famous wagon was loaded and ready.

Sunday, Dec 30th. Chimay was celebrating the departure the following morning of the founders of Caldey Abbey, Daughter House of Notre Dame de Scourmont. The High Mass was celebrated for them and by them, while after the office of Nones the Community enjoyed a general conversation together. (A rare thing.)

The following morning at 6 a.m. the 'Caldeyens' met in the cloisters, all carrying their hand luggage and dressed in the unusual attire of Clergymen, or—as the record has it—Gentlemen. At 9.45, a last meeting in the church, with prayers for the journey, ended with the Litany of the Saints and a procession, the new Caldey monks heading for the exit of the monastery carrying the Foundation Cross, while the rest of the Community returned to the church. At the door were the vehicles to take the travellers to Fourmies, where an express train was to be boarded for Calais. From here many of the party would make their first trip by sea. Fr Bernard had rejoined the Fathers, as he too was to be a founder monk.

The crossing was good and they were met by the Catholic priest at Dover, who welcomed them to England in the name of Cardinal Bourne. They were put on a slow train to London and arrived an hour late. At the Eccleston Hotel they were welcomed by Mgr Cardon de Wiart. After a night that had nothing in common with the silence of the monastery, the priests celebrated their Mass at Westminster Cathedral, or at the chapel of the Sisters of Charity, Carlisle St. After Mass, all had a substantial breakfast before beginning their tour of London. At Westminster Cathedral they were presented to Cardinal Bourne, who expressed his joy and hope in the new Cistercian foundation in Wales. The evening was spent quietly in the hotel and so the first day of 1929, and the first day in their new homeland, was over.

The following morning, Jan 2nd, 1929, the little colony left Paddington Station for the last stage of the journey. From Newport and Cardiff on they were looking for the sea, and after Swansea they hoped to catch a glimpse of Caldey—but in vain!

At last they reached Tenby, the station for Caldey, where the party was met by Fr Basil (already obviously well known there). A lorry was loaded with all the gear, while the monks walked to make their first contact with the town that would be their link with the mainland. Finally, the boat crossing to the Island—where the tide was so low that each monk was carried in turn on the back of a boatman, and gently put down on the Promised Land.

The entire population of Caldey, together with the advance party of Fr Rémy, Br Alberic and Br Andrew, were at the quay to meet the new Community. A procession was formed and the Litany of the Saints (interrupted as they left Chimay), was taken up again as the procession, headed by the Foundation Cross bearer, walked slowly to the church, where the monks took their places in the stalls. The bells rang out and the Te Deum was sung in joy and thanksgiving.

In the evening a fire was lit in the room to be used as a study room—it was cold and, of course, the wagon with so many necessary things had not yet arrived. In fact there had been a breakdown somewhere, and Fr Andrew Garcette had remained in London to investigate. Later each one retired to a cell to take some sleep on a straw mattress on the floor.

The regular monastic life was to begin on Jan 6th only, and until that time it was not necessary to keep the choral singing of the office, silence, and other obligations.

Thursday, Jan 3rd, was spent in visiting the various buildings, the lighthouse, the farm, the Old Priory, village church and excursions to points of interest on their new Island home. Such was the first contact with the Island that it conquered the hearts of all. 'True pearl of the Ocean', it has been said.

While the beauty of the Isle enchanted them, they were conscious of the work ahead when they examined the state of the farm buildings and the conditions to which they would have to adapt themselves. However, that did not discourage their young energy. They were ready to devote themselves to the re-establishment and the future prosperity of this monastic Island.

The following extract from the Caldey Island Journal gives a wonderful account of the initial impressions which the Island made on its new owners:

The Abbey

The monastery itself, built between 1910 and 1912 is situate almost in the centre of the Island, the buildings constructed from the stones quarried there, the walls covered with a white cement and the roof covered in red tiles. The total effect is very picturesque. The buildings form a quadrangle round which are to be found the various and necessary monastic places and offices. On the south side we find the lay brothers' quarters and the library. This side of the cloisters leads, at one end, to the sacristy, the church and the chapter house. At the other extremity it leads to the original Abbatial quarters with chapel, day-room, three bedrooms and bathroom. This is the part of the house which might in future be used as the monastery guesthouse. On the west side is found the refectory, the largest room in the house, complete with a pulpit for the reader. Beyond is the unusual octagonal kitchen, with scullery and small dining room. Beneath this part of the building we find the wardrobe, bakery and the laundry. On the north side, beneath the ground floor are workshops, paint store, central heating and a provision store room. On the ground floor itself are the offices of the cellarer and the secretary, the surgery, the calefactory, and the toilets. Off the north side cloister is the study room of the professed monks. On the first floor north side there are small bedrooms and a study room for juniors and novices.

The Farm

The farm is situated alongside the Old Priory church and much of it at first glance gave an impression of ruin and untidiness and provokes even a feeling of sadness. However, very quickly hope lifts up the spirits of a Cistercian—the agricultural monk!

Much of the material, too, was old and neglected and one can see the necessity for more modern equipment and as soon as possible, and much of the livestock would need replacing.

It is at the farm that is found the source of the most important commodity at Caldey—the spring of drinking water.

Before completing our inventory at the farm we noticed the presence of a large number of rats.

Furniture and moveable equipment etc.

For the new Community the bareness of the monastery was a major problem. Naturally, the old inhabitants had taken with them all moveable equipment for their new home while we, of course, had brought with us really only the bare necessities.

The church had the appearance of a Good Friday, naked and unadorned—and a sacristy of empty cupboards. The refectory was without chairs and the library was without books. For the cells, beds had to be taken provisionally from the Old Priory and some of the houses. Such are the early days of a foundation! But comfort was always round the corner with the thoughts of what was to be found when our wagon would be unloaded!

The wagon would contain the great choir books, monastic clothing for fifteen people, twenty-four chairs, stools for the refectory, linen and vestments for the church, together with crucifix and candle-sticks, two statues—St Benedict and St Bernard —kitchen utensils etc., books for the library, farm tools, to say nothing of some things added at the last moment to fill up some room left in the wagon—beans, plums, coffee and some Chimay beer!

Later we regretted, in view of the exchange rate, we had brought so little of everything!

January 4th was spent preparing the various rooms in the monastery to receive the content of the famous wagon—this dear wagon that is still waited for!

January 5th. The wagon arrived this afternoon, and so those things indispensable for us to begin the regular Cistercian life are here. A telegram was received from Rome announcing the Canonical Establishment of the Foundation on the morrow.

The Feast of the Epiphany of our Lord Jesus Christ—Jan 6th, 1929—was the official date of the Solemnisation of the Cistercian Foundation of Our Lady of Caldey.

All were in the church at 1 a.m. to the sound of the bells from the tower. The Little Office of Our Lady was recited, followed by meditation. At 2 a.m. the canonical night office was sung. Masses and the office of Prime followed. After Prime was held the first Chapter of the Cistercians of Caldey and the Rt Rev Dom Anselm le Bail, Abbot of Notre Dame de Scourmont announced in Latin, English and French the birth of the New Community. The list of offices was given together with the charges and tasks.

At the 7.30 a.m. Mass many of the islanders were present, and a sermon of welcome was preached by Fr Burke, an English priest. He wished all peace and happiness. Pontifical High Mass was celebrated by Dom Anselm and in spite of some difficulties the ceremonies and singing were well done.

Thanks to Brother cook and to his ingenuity an exceptionally good dinner was prepared. Vespers were sung during the afternoon, followed by Benediction, at which the islanders sang English hymns. The happy day ended with Compline and the solemn chant of the 'Salve Regina'.

So the regular life conforming to the Cistercian tradition began on January 6th, 1929, on the monastic Island of Caldey.

4
WHY DO MEN BECOME MONKS?

'Come ye yourselves apart into a desert place, and rest a while . . .
—And they departed into a desert place by ship privately.'
Mark 6 : 31-32.

So much, then, for the background to the coming of the present Community of monks to Caldey. Before trying to tell something of their story since that time, however, it would perhaps be as well to consider a monk's aims and beliefs to see whether we may achieve some sort of understanding of his problems and outlook on life. Or, in modern parlance, to find out 'what makes him tick.'

The outsider who would wish only to be charitable, rather than vicious, could be forgiven for looking upon him as some sort of 'nut case'. 'Drop out' is the more fashionable word. But at least, when a man gets up at quarter-past-three in the morning every day of his life and keeps going until bed-time he cannot be described as a 'lay-about.' His existence is indeed, by many standards, very hard. Yet the monk would probably not claim this to be so. He normally neither takes nor needs a holiday, and he is happy doing what he is doing.

To this extent society may well envy him. Most of us, even if we do not realise it, are ultimately in search of happiness. The monk, perhaps more so than most, has realised that peace of mind is true happiness, and that it is only to be found within him.

If we choose to seek happiness through the acquisition of material things, whether it be a bigger house, a better car, a job which offers security for our families, or any one of the many things which we fondly imagine could make a contribution towards our well-being, then that is our concern, our own problem and, as often as not, our misfortune. If a man sees things in an entirely different light and decides to become a monk, then that is his concern and not ours. It is hardly right for us to criticise or condemn him because he seeks his happiness in some other, harmless, way which is certainly in no competition with us.

By the standards of modern civilised society the life of a
monk could reasonably be classed as somewhat unnatural and,
certainly, by material standards, rather useless. But there are
now many serious minded people with sufficient intelligence
and concern for mankind who are increasingly voicing their
misgivings about the standards and the purpose of modern
civilised society. It would be purblind folly to assume that these
are necessarily the standards by which other ages or other
modes of life should be evaluated.

It is all too easy to ask what use a monk's vocation has. We
may as well ask, 'Why bother to paint a beautiful picture or
compose beautiful music?' If the answer should be that the
final creation remains to be enjoyed and appreciated by many
people, then it is also fair to point out that the reason for its
existence was the compelling urge of the artist or composer to
paint or compose it. Likewise, the monk knows his to be a true
vocation, although the ultimate value of it may need much
more examination in order to come to a fuller appreciation.

When we come to look more carefully at what is going on
around us we could question the usefulness of the vocations of
so many people who see themselves as indispensable pillars of
society. Some might go to say that possibly only doctors could
justifiably class themselves as really worthwhile and essential,
yet the naturist would immediately argue that doctors are the
most unnecessary section of society and point to the over-
crowded hospitals, the full waiting rooms and the huge
increase in the use of remedial drugs to suggest that the doctors
are failing rather than succeeding. Who, then, is to say what is
the use of any vocation?

We all need an individual peace with God and it is this for
which so many are yearning and searching. The welfare state
exerts a harsh tyranny and, as one wit has said, who wants to
win a rat race apart from the first rat? Concerned as we are with
our own welfare, with self and self-interest, we would all do
well to ask ourselves what the real usefulness of our own
existence is, before we decide we are in a position to criticise
the monks for the uselessness of theirs.

For those who want to give serious study to monasticism
there are hundreds of books available. This book does not
pretend to be such a study, but there are certain fundamentals

which need to be considered. The most frequently voiced criticism is that monks are in fact running away from life. The opposite is true. They are not running away, but going in search. They are going in search of God and there can be little doubt that they find Him. As Hubert Van Zeller writes in his book, *The Benedictine Idea*:

> By one and the same act monasticism offers holiness and demands it. Monasticism is prepared to discover to us the way, provided we take the direction indicated. It does not claim to be the only way, but it claims to be a sure way for those who are called to tread it. It does not claim to be the whole truth, but it points to the truth. It does not claim to be life itself, but it leads to life.

A monk hopes that by his way of life he will become sanctified and, through this, be able to intercede with God on behalf of his fellow-men. Some may well consider it to be a rather forlorn hope, but that is a monk's belief, and he is just as entitled to it as the man who believes that all his troubles will be ended if he can scoop the jackpot in the football pools. The monk aims to become one with God through Christ and thus, ultimately, to become one with his fellow-men, because 'the fulfilment of God in man is love.'

A sentence in Latin, often inscribed in some conspicuous part of Cistercian monasteries, has been translated:

> Here man more purely lives, less oft doth fall,
> More promptly rises, walks with stricter heed,
> More safely rests, dies happier, is freed
> Earlier from cleansing fires, and gains withal
> A brighter crown.

Monks, of course, are not the only people who seek solitude. Some farmers seek it. Mountaineers seek it. So do fishermen and those who go sailing. Let a man climb a high mountain, or sail single-handed round the world, and we honour him. He has proved what man can do, even though there may be no great point in it because usually it has been proved before. In the solitude, however, he finds something. Yet the monk, seeking God through solitude, is criticised. With such contradictions in men's thinking, we can understand why it must be difficult for the monk's purpose to be generally understood.

When their vocation is called into question it is usually part of the criticism that, if they feel that way about things, they should be out in the world doing something useful like tending the sick, feeding the poor, caring for the old, or anything else synonymous with Christian charity. As often as not, those who make such criticisms are the ones who are most occupied with their own affairs and do least for others, apparently oblivious to the fact that there is a crying need for such work because of the very ways of a civilisation of which they think so highly. On the other hand, those who do care for others are usually the last to offer such criticism.

It has been known, of course, for monks to fall by the wayside. It is one of the sadder facets of human nature that when such things happen they give rise to a measure of gloating, for people forget that there was only ever One who was perfect. It is true, too, that some seek to become monks because they are indeed running away or opting out, but they do not usually stay the course.

Christian monasticism dates from the fourth century and the conversion of the Roman Emperor Constantine to Christianity. For the three centuries up to this time the early Christians had been relentlessly persecuted. Those who had lived in the hills and caves and deserts had done so in order to survive. When Constantine put an end to Christian persecution it then became a case of the world becoming Christian and the Christians becoming worldly. Now, at last, they were allowed to take part in municipal and business affairs, and it was not long before some of them began to realise that they had lost something, and by means of monasticism were able to go in search of it. And the term 'Christians' is here meant to refer specifically to true followers of Christ as distinct from those who merely attend a place of worship.

It is here that we may have a slightly clearer understanding of a monk's purpose, for Jesus said, 'If thou wilt be perfect, go and sell that thou hast, and give to the poor, and thou shalt have treasure in heaven: and come and follow me.' On another occasion (and many people find it hard to understand and accept this), Jesus talked about leaving fathers and mothers and families, and followed it by saying, 'He that findeth his life shall lose it: and he that loseth his life for my sake shall find it.'

The monk, therefore, in his life of austerity, is denying himself what many believe to be the good things of life. He, too, believes marriage and family life to be good, he likes meat and good wine and he can have as keen an appreciation of anyone of the theatre or good music. He does not condemn these things, but denies himself them. Hence the belief that because he does not eat red meat he is a vegetarian. The vegetarian, in fact, either believes in the beneficial effects of such a diet or has some religious objection to the eating of food which has been prepared by slaughter. Unlike the monk, therefore, he is not denying himself anything by not eating meat.

This denying the self meat has been a form of penance since earliest Christian times, when meat was a more expensive food and thought of as being the food of the wealthier classes. The thinking is only the same as that which prompts the self-denial of meat or something else during Lent, or the eating of fish on a Friday as a reminder that it was on that day that Christ died. In our own time turkey was once regarded as a special luxury for the better-off at Christmas time, and chicken, too, was something beyond the means of the less privileged. Factory farming, with its conveyor-belt production, has altered all that, coupled with increased living standards all round, but Christmas is still thought of as a time for poultry.

When the monk is ill he is allowed to eat meat. On the odd occasion, when affairs necessitate his mixing with the rest of the world, he is not being a hypocrite when, away from his vocation, he joins with those with whom he comes in contact, by eating meat or drinking alcohol in moderation.

At various time throughout the centuries, monasticism, like civilisation itself, has taken wrong turnings. Monks have become involved in political power and intrigue and they have become established as feudal landlords. Even where they have founded seats of learning, or become involved in hospital work, which society has seen as commendable, this has distracted them from their true vocation of monasticism. At other periods some of them have become lax in their ways and indulged in easy living, being content to beg and live on charity. Always, therefore, there has been a heavy responsibility on the leaders of monastic life to direct the movement along the right lines, moving with the times, but avoiding dangers inherent in a situation when they are, as it were, in the world but not of it. Whatever their success may appear to be when judged by worldly standards, if they fail in their true vocation then anything else is meaningless.

One of the reasons for the foundation of the Cistercian Order was the desire to get away from grandeur and ostentation. The clothes adopted by the Cistercians were of the cheapest material, in the form of a white wool habit and black hood. Hence they became known as the 'white monks'. They still followed the Rule of St Benedict and continue to do so. Indeed, with their often charming sense of humour, they might even say that Benedictines profess the Rule of St Benedict, but Cistercians follow it.

The monks read a part of the Holy Rule every day. Apart from any bearing it has on monasticism, it is in itself fascinating reading, and in it is found the clue to the entire pattern of a monk's life and the ambition which leads him to take such a path, which he sees as the closest possible following of Christ. This is the whole emphasis of his vocation. The Rule is austere, but not merely for austerity's sake. Based entirely on, and interpreting, the Scriptures, it is full of wisdom and kindliness, and it soon becomes evident that Benedict's first priority is the love of God and all mankind. If austerity contributes to this and helps to make it possible, so be it.

'Idleness is an enemy of the soul...' so that the monk, according to the Rule, occupies himself in the labour of his hands. By tradition the monks become farmers, for the Rule says:

> If the needs of the place, or their poverty, oblige them to labour themselves at gathering in the crops let them not be saddened thereat, because then are they truly Monks, when they live by the labour of their hands, as did our fathers and the Apostles. Yet let all be done with moderation, on account of the faint-hearted.

Over the years the Cistercians cleared swamps, reclaimed land and improved it, and frequently set in motion habits of good husbandry which others were able to follow to advantage. So it was that Wordsworth was able to write:

The potent call
Doubtless shall cheat full oft the heart's desires;
Yet, while the rugged Age on pliant knee
Vows to rapt Fancy humble fealty
A gentler life spreads round the holy spires;
Where'er they rise, the sylvan waste retires,
And aery harvests crown the fertile lea.

The modern Cistercian monk retains some of the normal ties of life, being visited by his family, and receiving and writing letters. However, as with a student in college, who really applies himself to his studies, the period of trial and testing proves to be more strict. The novice makes his first, or simple, profession after two years, and at the end of five years he makes his final, or solemn, profession. It is then that he makes his solemn declaration of renunciation of entitlement to all goods and money and gives them all away 'to be poor with the poor Christ.' From now on he has no personal possessions and has become one of a complete family who share everything.

It is part of his life, too, to submit himself in complete obedience. In accordance with this vow he will perform without question whatever task the Abbot calls upon him to perform. It could be, for example, that a parish priest is ill and a request is sent to the monastery to send a member of their Community, some of whom will be ordained priests, on 'supply'. The Abbot will ask one of the Brothers to undertake this task, and it would never occur to this monk to reply that if he had seen his vocation as a parish priest he would not have become a monk in the first place. He accepts this duty without question, just as he will turn to baking bread or sweeping the floor and even, in some cases, find himself being transferred to another Community whose numbers have become so depleted as to threaten its existence.

It will thus be appreciated that, as the monks' spiritual and temporal leader, a great deal of responsibility rests upon the Abbot. The affairs of the monastery are discussed in Chapter by all the members, when everyone may speak freely, and the Abbot, who is elected by the members in a straightforward democratic election, will take their deliberations into account and be guided by them when making any decision.

Contrary to popular belief, the Cistercians do not take any vow of silence. If they have something to say, they say it. At the same time, there is no idle chatter, and they value very highly the power of silence to keep them in the presence of God, and give Him the opportunity to speak to them. During the six hours after rising at 3.15 a.m. the monastery becomes a place of pronounced peace and quiet, and, where it will suffice, the monks are content to communicate with each other by hand signals.

To those who imagine the life of a monk to be slow-moving, it possibly comes as a surprise to see him walking quickly 'with the speedy step of obedience.' This is part of his way of life, as it is also to walk with head bent down and eyes fixed on the earth as a sign of humility, and 'always saying in his heart what the publican in the Gospel said with his eyes fixed on the earth: 'Lord, I a sinner am not worthy to raise mine eyes to Heaven.' And again, with the prophet: 'I am bowed down and humbled on every side.'

By 3.30 in the morning the monk is in chapel for a half-hour's service of psalms and lessons. There are no fewer than seven services, or offices, some of them lasting no more than ten minutes each, during the day, with Mass being celebrated at 6.30. And the Mass is the focal point of the monk's life of prayer, just as it is the focal point of the Catholic Faith.

The emphasis on prayer and devotion is in these first hours of the day, because then the mind is quiet and open, and at its most alert. At 6 o'clock, before Mass, there has been a half-hour's silent meditation which can take place anywhere. Usually it is in the church, but it may be in the cloisters, or even in the garden. A light breakfast is taken at 7 o'clock, dinner at 12.30, and supper at 6.30. During dinner, which has been prepared by one of the monks and served by two others, a monk will read aloud while the remainder eat in silence. The last office of the day, Compline, is at 7.30 p.m. and the monks retire to their cubicles for the night at 8 o'clock. For much of the day they will have been engaged in manual work, some of it very heavy, and, should they ever permit themselves a self-satisfied thought, they might well, with Longfellow's 'Village Blacksmith' in mind, say to themselves, 'Something attempted, something done, has earned a night's repose.'

5
FARMING DEPRESSION—THE EARLY YEARS

'In the sweat of thy face shalt thou eat bread...': Genesis 3: 19

The problems of farming an island, and the agricultural trends of this particular period, have been dealt with in detail elsewhere.* It may be useful, however, to make some reference to them here if we are to appreciate the struggle which faced the monks in their new home, committed as they were to supporting themselves financially, and doing so, not only by means of farming when the economic climate was so serious, but on an island with all its attendant difficulties and extra costs.

When the Cistercians came to Caldey, it will be remembered from the brief inventory in the Journal already referred to, they took over the fifty milking cows from the Benedictines. In 1928 that was a fair-sized herd. But the reference to the dilapidated state of the farm and buildings is also worth remembering.

If it is said that the Benedictines had not been farming the Island very well, this is not in any way to be critical of their efforts. It was a time when the better a man farmed the more money he lost. The best he could hope to do was to survive somehow until times improved and, quite frequently, this meant neglecting the hedges and boundary walls, ploughing no land and spending no money on fertilisers. There was no point in producing something which either could only be sold at a loss or, worse still, not sold at all.

Until this time the traditional produce of Pembrokeshire's farms had been cattle and fat lambs for the butcher. Dairy produce was mainly for sale to meet the limited demand in the county. Until the advent of the internal combustion engine, only those farmers living close enough to a railway station, and able to deliver their milk there by horse and cart, were able to take advantage of this method of transport.

With the coming of motorised transport, however, more and more farmers began to turn from beef to milk, which could now

---

* *The Sounds Between.*

be transported to the railway stations for sale to the wholesalers in the industrial towns of South Wales. But this, too, could be a precarious business. The less scrupulous firms would sometimes fail to pay a producer, and then start buying from someone else. When they went bankrupt, as some of them did, the farmer to whom they owed money did not even have the hope of prolonged and costly legal action to recover it. Sometimes, when they had more milk than they needed, they would return a farmer's milk to him on the grounds that it was sour, safe in the knowledge that by the end of the return railway journey it would be sour anyway. It was not until the formation of the Milk Marketing Board in 1933 that stability was made possible through organised marketing and the guarantee of the monthly milk cheque. This life-line, however, was to be of no avail to an island farmer.

At this period, such was the depression in the industry, farmers sometimes had nothing else to do but bury butter which they were unable to sell. Fat cattle and lambs could only be sold at ruinous prices. For the farmer on the island the position was far worse. He had the extra cost, to say nothing of the difficulty and risk, of transporting all his requirements across a stretch of water in a small, open boat. Sometimes the elements would make the crossing hazardous, and sometimes impossible. There would be the extra cost and difficulty to get his cattle and produce to the mainland, where it would fetch no more than the same inadequate price as that received by the mainland farmer. Indeed, the island farmer was even worse off, because it was out of the question for him to bring his stock home in the hope that it might sell better next time. The marketing of vegetables and greenhouse produce was just as precarious.

The efforts of the Benedictines must be judged against this background. At the same time it must be borne in mind that the farm on Caldey was not large enough to support a Community of about twenty people, which it was now being called upon to do.

When Aelred Carlyle left Caldey in 1921 the monks were already in a parlous state financially. He had tried all sorts of crazy ideas for making money, all short-lived and usually disastrous, without establishing anything of any permanence.

The two Cistercian monks, who had gone to the Island as 'bailiffs' when the Order bought Caldey and its livestock in 1925, had, no doubt, with their own knowledge of farming, been a helpful influence, and efforts were being made to put the farming business on a sound footing. They were even keeping milk records, which was very enterprising at that time, under the aegis of the old Pembrokeshire Milk Recording Society.

On the farm, the Cistercians carried on where the Benedictines had left off. The cows were Dairy Shorthorns, a useful dual-purpose breed, but due soon to be superseded as the national dairy cow by the heavier-milking British Friesian. With the establishment of the Milk Marketing Board in 1933 and the benefits it brought to the milk producer it became less sensible than ever to produce butter for sale. The price obtainable for a pound of butter bore no relationship whatsoever to the worth of the milk used to make it. It was therefore much better to sell the liquid milk and, in addition to getting a better price for it in this way, it saved the work involved in making the butter. There was a revolution in the countryside as lorries carrying milk churns became an increasingly familiar sight. But no milk lorry called on Caldey!

Milk could be fed to pigs, but there was no great future in this either, when pigs lost more money for a man than almost anything else he could keep. Eventually, therefore, the monks gave up producing milk and turned instead to using a bull of a beef breed on their cows in order to produce beef. Occasionally at that time cattle were crossed to to the mainland by swimming them behind the boat, and landing on the sands near Giltar Point at the far end of Tenby's South Beach. This, as can easily be imagined, was a hazardous operation.

The Journal, which recorded something of the monks' affairs during their earlier years on Caldey, dealt with many items which would hardly be regarded as being of any great moment. There were also many references to arrivals and departures of various monks, visiting dignitaries, ordinations and professions. But there were occasional references, too, to matters concerning the farm, and to quote a few of these at random may be to paint the picture more clearly than would be possible in many words.

1929

Jan. 10. Manual work: Everyone worked on the task of carrying stones from a crumbling wall in the village to the site near St David's Church where it will be necessary to build an enclosure wall. Today a number of letters arrived from Chimay.

Jan. 20. Week passed in regular life—everyone working in the afternoons on clearing the fields of stones to prepare for manuring.

Feb.16. Saturday: No boat since last Monday. It rains, it snows, it is freezing!

April 25. Arrival of two new cows to add to the herd. The means of transport was a raft towed by the boat!

June 13. Return of Br Christopher with his nephew Felix Vincent. Caldey was very happy to welcome back this man particularly precious to her with so much work to be done. He was a joiner and would be assisted by his nephew in this department. The Abbot announced that Br Christopher would be Sub-Cellarer with special duties at the farm and also Sub-Master of Lay Brothers.

Sept. 27. *The fire on the Caldey Boat—the Teresina.*

In order to assist the departure of visitors to Caldey the boat was to have been floated at about three in the morning. About half—past midnight the coastguard telephoned Caldey that the boat was on fire outside the harbour. The following morning a team of monks went over to rescue what they could, and the motor was salvaged.

What now to do without a boat? The boatmen of Tenby immediately offered to put themselves at our disposal. However, after a week it was realised that one boat ought to be the property of the monastery and that its service must be independent. The engine of the 'Teresina' had suffered little damage and was a good one, but the body was not the best for this part of the world and with the least wind made embarking and disembarking quite dangerous.

1930

June 24. Everyone at the haymaking under the direction of the Abbot.

July 4. New boat the 'Iolanthe' brought in from Pembroke Dock after a rough trip of six hours.

Sept. 27. Afternoon—the last sheaves of oats were brought in and threshed.

Dec. 15. Transport of two young horses from Saundersfoot, where they have a crane, by boat to Caldey. A crane situated on the quay at Caldey would facilitate loading and off-loading.

1931

March 9. South-east wind and no boat for nine days. This is the longest period without contact with the mainland. 'Obeata Solitudo. . . Sola beatitudo!'

April 9. The horse 'Darling' has left the pasture of Caldey by the fatal boat that leads to the abattoir. For years he had grazed on the soft grass in complete liberty and freedom from care. Old as Melchisedech—as no one knows his age! [Skin brought a few shillings to the finances of the monastery.]

1932

Feb. 24 Very heavy snow fall—all is white. The snow continues to fall during the day. Telephone communication off. Boat (engine) failed to start.

It will be seen from these various references that, in addition to the difficult farming times, there were many other problems with which the monks had to contend.

Within four days of the official establishment of this foundation there is the reference which emphasises the degree of priority given to the monastic life in the carrying of stones to build an enclosure. In spite of the great expenditure which had been involved in the building of the monastery, it was still necessary to build an enclosure wall which was essential to Cistercian observance. The worldly or practical man would no doubt say that priority should have been given to the more immediate need of the farm in order to 'generate cash flow.' But these men had gone to Caldey to live the life of Cistercian monks, and we have seen something of what that involves and why they do it. Nothing must be allowed to come between them and their search for God, and yet, within the first week, worldly demands could have distracted them from their true purpose. A small and unimportant instance, it is true, but it is worth recording as it helps to make more readily understandable something of what is happening in the context of today's almost frightening pressures. There has always been this need to balance the demands of their monastic life and the need to pay their way in a fiercely competitive commercial society.

Ten days later they are found clearing stones from the fields as part of their application to farming. Some of these stones would have been used to repair the field walls, and the better ones for the building of the enclosure.

A month later we find an example of what the weather can do
to anyone trying to earn a living by farming an island. For a
week there had been no boat. What could this mean in terms of
hard cash if there were cattle or fat lambs ready for market,
fresh butter, eggs, or garden produce packed and ready to be
taken to the mainland, butchers having to buy animals for
slaughter elsewhere at short notice, shop-keepers finding
themselves without produce which they had been expecting
and had been promised? They could be forgiven if they decided
to find a more reliable source of supply by next time.

Always, too, there is the problem of finding, and the cost of
maintaining, a suitable and reliable boat, and there is the
question of communication. Originally a telephone cable had
been run along the sea-bed, but when this was broken in 1938
by the action of the sea wearing it on the rocks, it was not
replaced, and there was no telephone until a radio telephone,
the first in the country, was installed in 1951.

Amidst all these problems, however, one thing is certain. The
monks know that if they are to be free to follow their vocation,
then the problems have to be solved. In many ways they are, in
the modern idiom, on a hiding to nothing. If they fail, then
their critics can say they should have got on with doing a job of
work the same as anybody else. If they succeed, then the critics
can discourse freely on the hypocrisy of their willingness to
engage in commercial enterprise when they are supposed to
have turned their backs on the world. Better, however, to
succeed and remain to be criticised, than to fail and be ridiculed.

The Community took some time to solve their problems, but
eventually established themselves securely in their new home.
How they did it has its place later in the story.

6
A TIME OF MISCHIEF

'We are troubled on every side, yet not distressed; we are perplexed, but not in despair; persecuted, but not forsaken; cast down, but not destroyed': 2 Corinthians 4:8-9.

According to the reader's personal sympathy, or any affinity with the previous Order of monks on Caldey, it may may have been thought that references in the first chapter to Aelred Carlyle's affairs could and should have been omitted. At this point, however, the reason for their inclusion becomes more obvious, because what had been happening on Caldey for more than two decades before the coming of the Cistercians had had considerable influence on what people in Tenby and the surrounding area thought of monks in general and Caldey monks in particular.

The Cistercians were obviously going to need the goodwill of their mainland neighbours, but who on the mainland could be expected to know that the newcomers would not be content to beg, but, by long tradition, were committed to supporting themselves by their own manual labour? To make matters even more difficult for them, they were foreigners and Catholics at a time when both were suspect, and their lack of knowledge of the English language made communication so much more difficult. Moreover, by the very nature of their calling, and the silence they observed, they found little opportunity to learn the new language.

As if this were not enough, more trouble was to be created for them after their arrival. The first of these resulted from the actions of one man, the repercussions of which did a great deal to harm the monks. There is insufficient evidence to be able to attribute motive, but the result was abundant proof that Major Robert James de Carteret O'Neill was a rogue. With the wisdom which comes so easily with hindsight it is clear from as early as his first letter that the man was bogus. It all started in the autumn of 1930, when a parish priest wrote to say that he had a friend, who, after much trouble and sorrow, was becoming a convert to the Holy Church. The idea was that he should go into a quiet retreat for a couple of months in order to write and prepare himself for reception, and the priest no doubt felt fully justified in adding, 'He is altogether a most desirable convert and will be of great help with his pen later on.'

The copy of the monks' reply, in faded pencil, is worth recording, particularly bearing in mind the reference to language difficulties. The original also shows many crossings out and corrections in search of the right word. It read as follows:

'We should willingly accept your friend who is proposed a holiday for four or five weeks but we find a difficulty for food. As you know we have no custom to eat meat and our cook does not know well to prepare it. If your friend is satisfied with the food prepared for the community with some extra (bacon and meat from time to time) we can accept and receive him. 5 shillings per day, if this diet is not suitable to live it should be better to him to stay at the Old Priory House (Manageress Miss Grossé).'

The three Misses Grossé, aunts of one of the monks at Chimay, had come to Caldey in the spring of 1930 and ran the guest-house at the Old Priory. Not long after he arrived on the Island, O'Neill opted for the comfort and more substantial fare which they provided.

By the spring of the following year he had produced a book called *A Modern Pilgrimage*, which told of his journey to Caldey, the life of a monk and his own thoughts for the future. It was published by the Priory Publishing Company, Caldey, a company of his own creation. The factory of the Mayflower Press, Plymouth, who printed the book, was bombed during the war and all their records were destroyed, so that there is no way of knowing who paid their bill. It is a fair guess that the monks would have done so. A number of pictures of the author appeared in the book but, in each of them, he had his back to the camera. He presented the monastery with a finial cross and silver communion plate, and performed other munificent deeds. Then he went to Ireland to the monastery at Mount Melleray.

By the time the bills for his charitable deeds towards various people, as well as those for the finial cross and communion plate, began to arrive, he had left Mount Melleray and was only making sporadic contact through intermediaries. Solicitors and creditors wrote in vain to O'Neill at Caldey, and then addressed themselves to the Father Prior. Without hesitation, the monks explained the position, which was nothing to do with them, and, poor as they were, paid the bills. It is a pattern which has been repeated many times over the years.

There has never been any shortage of those willing to take advantage of the monks' simple and trusting nature, just as there have always been those, no matter what they lacked by the way of qualifications, ready to urge them to embark on all sorts of ridiculous schemes. This latter aspect was dealt with very succinctly by Peter Anson in *Abbot Extraordinary* when writing of the state of affairs before ever the Cistercians came to Caldey. He wrote:

> The various and often pathetic schemes to add to the earned income of the Community devised by Abbot Aelred are worth mentioning, because they do show he tried all sorts of ways and means. Between 1914 and 1919 he belonged to the Country Gentleman's Association and used to consult this organization frequently about the farm and market gardens. It was the Dowager Lady Bute who advised him to grow certain medicinal herbs, the importing of which from abroad had ceased by the war. This new Island industry was given up after a brief trial. Another friend persuaded him to invest in a printing press, but it was never used, and the bits and pieces lay neglected in one of the workshops. Somebody else must have told him that there was a good market for alabaster lamp-shades and flower-bowls. Then came the setting up of a workshop for making stone crosses, holy water stoups and bird baths. The stained glass factory, started in 1915, produced no more than three windows, and they remained in the monastery. Pheasant breeding, so a certain visitor maintained, would prove to be most profitable. The result was that our Abbot engaged a gamekeeper, and bought some birds, and was thus able to get in some shooting himself. One day it was decided that a special brand of cheese would bring in big profits. The necessary outfit was installed in the dairy, but this project was abandoned after a 'Caldey Cheese' had been sampled.
>
> Then came the goats. Another visitor assured our Abbot that they would be in every way admirable. Caldey was 'just the place for them'—perfect climate, good pasturage, etc., etc. The Abbot

must write to the Goat Club, which would be able to supply
anything required. 'Togenburg billies, Anglo-Nubian nannies,
whatever he fancied.' Acting on this advice, a letter was dictated
to the Secretary of the Goat Club. The reply came 'with a lovely
heraldic device on the notepaper—argent a billy goat trottant,
horned and hoofed proper, with a true lover's knot.' But it was a
shock to read that the Club did not know anything about goats in
spite of its name—its sole purpose was to provide social amenities
for officers of the Royal Navy who found themselves in London.
Later our Abbot did introduce a herd of goats, but unfortunately
they did not make the 'pot of money' which had been predicted by
his enthusiastic visitor. In spite of their wonderful up-to-date
incubators the hens were almost as unhelpful as the goats and
pheasants in achieving a balanced monastic economy, granted
that the eggs did help to reduce the grocer's bills, and added to the
variety of our meals, after the no-cooking diet had been given up.

It was another day, another age, but the pattern remained
the same when O'Neill lit upon the Cistercians. There is no
record of his showing anybody how to make money, but there
is ample record of his ability to relieve them of it. Although
there have been many other such cases, of varying degrees of
seriousness, mention is made of this one because of the effect
it had at the time on the monks' good name. O'Neill had
represented himself on the mainland as a member of the
Community and, when word went round amongst the trades-
people, it began to look like the same story of financial
irresponsibility all over again. It did the monks no good at all.

Then, other stories of his behaviour came to light. The guest-
house where O'Neill had been staying was attached to the Old
Priory. Around the turn of the century a legend had been born
relating to hidden treasure and a Black Monk. Briefly, the story
went that a monk had brought gold plate and gold altar vessels
to Caldey from Glastonbury to ensure that they did not fall into
the hands of Henry VIII. When, in due course, the Caldey
monastery was also endangered, the monk hid the treasure and
bricked himself in and died with it. The hiding place remained
unknown until O'Neill, believing the story to be true, tried to
find it.

In all probability he came to Caldey merely to use it as a
vehicle for his book, and for various articles which he wrote,

and only heard this little bit of local nonsense after his arrival. The inherent dishonesty of the man was sufficient to ensure that he would do some searching. He dug into the wall of the room where he had been doing his writing and left the place in a chaotic state.

During this time O'Neill had charmed the Misses Grossé into entrusting him with some three hundred pounds which he was to invest very advantageously for them. This disappeared with him when he did his proverbial and literal 'moonlight flit', never more to set foot on Caldey. It is said that the police eventually caught up with him and that he received an eighteen months' prison sentence under his real name of James Drummond (both the name O'Neill and his rank being spurious), but considerable research has not so far resulted in confirmation of this. Good Catholics will no doubt be relieved to know that neither is there any record of his becoming a convert.

The most distressing problem of all, however, was the deliberate irritation and trouble which were constantly being created by one of the Island residents, Mrs King, a lapsed Catholic, who was to remain as an embarrassing element for the next twenty years. The monks, who believe in meeting such behaviour with kindness, will only say in their charitable way, 'She was good in many ways and we all have our weaknesses.' The facts are, however, that she went out of her way to make trouble and she caused the Prior many sleepless nights. In an area of predominantly Protestants and Welsh Nonconformists there was no shortage of bigotry and animosity, and she found willing helpers.

To understand why she was on Caldey and in a position to make a nuisance of herself it is necessary to give a few details of her background. Originally she had helped Helen Hope, who ran a drama school in Bath for the encouragement of amateurs. Miss Hope was a charming woman of considerable wealth, a devout Anglican and much interested in the monastic experiment being conducted by the plausible Carlyle, who presumably had little difficulty in persuading her to pour money into his venture. In return he allowed her the tenancy of a house on Caldey with a far-reaching agreement.

Consuela Mary de Reyes, who had become Miss Hope's assistant, subsequently married Peter King, Miss Hope's chauffeur/gardener. When Miss Hope died in 1923 she had left everything to Mrs King, who had claimed that this included the rights given to Miss Hope by the Benedictines over the holiday house on Caldey. She had been living there for six years by the time the Cistercians arrived. From the outset Mrs King behaved very thoughtlessly. The Cistercians, in an attempt to avoid friction, gave way. Mrs King, however, used the house in the most inconsiderate way possible, giving large, noisy parties on Sundays which went on until late at night in the house and garden situated right beneath the monastery walls, and was known to have circulated misleading or false reports on the mainland. The outcome was an unworthy chapter in the history of the press when, in August 1932, J.C. Griffith Jones, a reporter from the *Western Mail*, went over to Caldey and misrepresented himself as an archaeologist.

He made no attempt to approach the monks at the monastery, where he could have been given all the information he required, and would have been hospitably received. Aided by Mrs King, his chief source of information, he wrote a series of three articles which were, for the most part, derogatory. He made a number of sneering references to these foreigners who now sought to deny good Welshmen the right to enter upon their native soil, and spoke of the *iron rule* which the benign Fr Basil imposed upon the Islanders. And all this innuendo was directed at kind and inoffensive men who had written in their Journal a few years previously, not about arriving in a foreign land, but of their feelings on arriving 'in their new homeland.'

The *Western Mail* heralded this epic, in their issue of August 31st 1932, under double headlines:

CALDEY—ISLE OF MYSTERY. WESTERN MAIL MAN'S ADVENTURES.
Just off Tenby and the historic South Pembrokeshire coast—'Little England Beyond Wales'—Caldey, 'Island of Saints', is still the most mysterious isle in Britain.
Only three miles from the mainland, it has become the property of French Trappist monks from Chimay Abbey, Belgium, and is said to be ruled by 'an iron Cistercian hand'—a Hush-hush Island!
Thousands of visitors go to Caldey from Tenby as day-trippers each summer, but few penetrate the inner circle of the Mystery Isle.

In tomorrow's *Western Mail* the first of three special articles
telling the inner story of Caldey will appear.

It will be the first-hand account by a *Western Mail* man who
learnt many of the Island's secrets, talked to villagers and monks,
landed on Sunday—the forbidden day for visitors, and stayed a
night at Caldey after being submitted to searching questions
followed by an S.O.S. to the mainland police three miles away.

Order your copy of tomorrow's *Western Mail* now.

As a result of these articles there was considerable correspondence, to which the *Western Mail* allowed Griffith Jones
himself to reply. The Community, of course, had no member to
speak or write fluently for them, and so Fr Ivor Daniel, the
Roman Catholic priest at Pembroke Dock and a good friend of
the monks, took it upon himself to write on their behalf, with
the approval of the Prior, Fr Aelred Lefevre. The *Western Mail*
carried Fr Daniel's letter, but with a footnote to the effect that
it had been abbreviated owing to considerations of space. It
may well be thought that it was a pity that the same considerations had not applied to the diatribe which had prompted it in
the first place.

Copies of the letter were sent to *The Tenby Observer* and *The
Catholic Herald*, both of which carried the letter in full. *The
Catholic Herald*, however, printed in italics those parts of the
letter which the *Western Mail* had omitted 'owing to
considerations of space.' This in itself was an indictment, and
demonstrated clearly the bias against the monks.

In some ways, however, in its repercussions and amongst
thinking people, this episode may well have done the monks
some good. The letter, as published in the two other papers,
was a faithful reproduction of the original, which is still in the
monastery archives, and being able to read, in their proper
context, those parts which the *Western Mail* had suppressed,
enabled people to see, not only a lack of fairness towards the
monks, but something of the ethos of the monastic Community.
As Fr Daniel had said in his original letter:

> If the reporter gets into Heaven, as he says, more easily than he
> got into Caldey, he will be a lucky man.
> But he must not go as an archaeologist. Truth is necessary there.

There are real mysteries and secrets on the Island but not observable by one to whom

A primrose by the river's brim
A yellow primrose is to him
And nothing more.

Every grain of sand on the 'lonely' Priory Bay, every flower in the 'crannied wall', every life, death, joy, sorrow, pain, evil deeds and good, they are all mysteries compared with which the lives of the monks are but a trifling thing.

That is no mystery at all to him who can discern the things that are to the peace of men, but of which eyes of flesh see nothing, and to which the writer of the articles was spiritually blind.

Whatever good, if any, may have come from all this, the monks naturally found it hurtful and distressing, whilst Mrs King remained undeterred. She found a ready ally in the *Western Mail*. Four years later, in the summer of 1936, the story of the arrogance and perfidy of these foreign religious exploded and reached the pages of almost every national newspaper. Before giving a brief account of this episode, mention must be made of an important occurrence in the story of Cistercian Caldey.

In January 1932, Patrick Moore had been received into the Order as a postulant-lay-brother. In September of the same year he was clothed as Br Thomas. Two years later, on Sept 29th, 1934, the simple entry in the Journal reads:

At last! The first profession of an English novice—Br Thomas.

On October 27th, 1935, he was put in charge of 'the Island, the boat and all the liaison with business outside.'

It was Cliff Gladwin, the Derbyshire fast bowler, in a Test match crisis in South Africa, when England needed one run to win off the last ball of the match, who said, 'Cometh the hour, cometh the man.'

Br Thomas was destined to become a legend in his own lifetime. When he died, suddenly and tragically, at the age of fifty-seven in 1966, it cast a gloom over the town of Tenby, and the Town Council postponed their meeting for a day. Such had been his work over the previous thirty years that, by that time, it would have been difficult indeed for anyone to have been able to beat up a story against the monks amongst the people of Tenby. Perhaps this was his greatest achievement in life, and the general recognition of it his most fitting memorial. Subsequently, as a mark of the towns-people's respect and affection for him, the Tenby Rotary Club opened a garden of rest in his memory.

But that was thirty years on. By the time Br Thomas had taken over as the Community's mainland steward in the autumn of 1935 there had been a steady increase in the number of summer day-visitors landing on the Island, and all sorts of problems were arising. The summer before the Cistercians took over, a gang of trippers had gone through the greenhouses like a tornado, tearing down peach trees and grape-vines, and smashing the glass. A tightening up in control, with no policeman or anyone else to help, was essential. In the spring of 1936, Br Thomas convened a meeting between the Tenby boatmen and a sub-committee of the Town Council at which certain problems were discussed, and a code of conduct readily agreed to, concerning the management of boats and people. In the summer the Prior put up a notice to this effect in the Island post office. Amongst other things there would continue to be no landing of visitors on Sunday, and the 'season' would close for the Tenby boatmen on October 12th.

The Islanders, too, recognised that all this would be to their advantage, and agreed to it readily. It would be to nobody's detriment. Apart, that is, from Mrs King, who saw that it would effectively put a stop to some of her nonsense. It was unfortunate that one of the boatmen at that time was also adept at stirring up trouble. Amongst other things, he spread the rumour that the monks were now going to restrict the use of the Caldey foreshore, and confine visitors to crossing only in the monks' own boat. It was only later that this falsehood came to light and was refuted.

Once the 'Ordinance', as it soon came to be referred to, was put up in the post office, Mrs King sent a copy to the *Western Mail*. Letters began to appear in the press, the Tenby boatmen were persuaded that their livelihood was being threatened and, on August 20th, the *Western Mail* published a letter from Mrs King. In the same edition they devoted part of their Editorial column to this burning issue and, with a superb disregard for the facts, they talked about citizens' rights, free navigation, and His Majesty's lieges on lawful errand, and finally suggested that, because of its strategic position 'at the mouth of Milford Haven and also commanding the entrance to the Bristol Channel' (an odd sense of geography) 'the Home Office and the military authorities should give attention to these matters and that courts of justice should be formally asked to define and uphold the rights of the public.'

The monastery Journal carries the following brief entry for the following day, August 21st, 1936:

> Visit of the Chief of Police for Pembrokeshire sent by the Home Office (Sir John Simon) as a result of statements made against the Community. He left the Island very satisfied and much more favourable towards Caldey than when he arrived.

When it had been made to appear that the Tenby boatmen were to be deprived of their livelihood, they found a ready champion (much too ready) in Colonel Hugo Allen of Tenby. It is said that the worst thing you can say about a man is that he means well. Be that as it may, Col Allen meant well. A decent man, with a warm regard for the boatmen, he was the sort who acted first and thought afterwards. On August 30th, ten days after the *Western Mail's* Editorial comment, the gallant Colonel, in the presence of suitably-briefed photographers and reporters, stage-managed a landing on Caldey on a Sunday afternoon, accompanied by his wife and the daughter of the then Rector of Tenby, and defied Br Thomas and all comers to remove him.

For September 8th, the entry in the monastery Journal reads:

> Tenby refuses Caldey tomatoes under the pretext that the Community was in competition with the Tenby producers. Matter discussed by the Tenby Council.

Col Allen was a member of this body.

J. C. Griffith Jones, now employed by the *News Chronicle*, was somehow slow off the mark. Not until September 11th did a piece appear under his name. Having admitted that he had been unable to find any evidence to prove that the Community imposed a permanent ban upon visitors, he contented himself with his usual references to an alien Community setting themselves up as dictators on a British island, to the fact that the monastery had been built with Anglican funds, to the claim that a Celtic chapel on the Island should be scheduled as an ancient monument with a right of way established for the people, and to the occasion when a woman who had a house on the Island (who else but Mrs King?) had wanted to cross when the monastery boat was not available.

A week previously, the *Western Mail* had quoted from the Tenby *Parish Magazine* in which the Rector, Canon Bickerton Edwards, whose daughter had landed on Caldey with Col Allen, had written what he possibly supposed was the final adjudication on the matter. He started off by saying:

> Our foreign neighbours on the Island of Caldey are evidently jealous of their rights of ownership. They have thought it necessary to assert them very emphatically of late, with the unfortunate result that their friendly relationship with the citizens of Tenby is considerably affected.

It possibly came as a surprise in some quarters when it was realised that the monks had some reasonable people amongst their friends. These included Wafter Roach, a wealthy lawyer and former M.P. for Pembrokeshire, and his wife, who had a house on the Island. They wrote sensible, well-reasoned letters to the press explaining the true position. Then, on September 11th, the *Tenby Observer* appeared with a leading article very much in support of the monks. The Editor, R. L. C.Morrison, was one of those who had had first-hand experience of the integrity of the monks in settling accounts incurred by Major O'Neill. The article is perhaps worth quoting in full.

> We hold no brief for the Caldey Community, but a sense of fair play suggests that their action in asserting their rights of ownership is being distorted in certain quarters. What the monks have done to protect the peace and privacy of the Island is only natural. Surely the implication that they desire to live in complete seclusion so that they can better carry on 'secret plotting' has no foundation! What is the nature of their 'plots'? One correspondent recently suggested that these alleged machinations were political, and implied that religion was but a cloak to camouflage their sinister

import. We consider such views puerile, without a scintilla of evidence to support them, and they may be dismissed as moonshine. We are certain that behind the recent action of the Community there lies no motive beyond that of preserving the peace and seclusion of Caldey. It was purchased for the purpose of a religious retreat—a place in which men of high ideals could—the world forgotten and by the world forgot—engage in spiritual devotions. The chain of prayer is unbroken—hour after hour it goes on with changes of supplicants, right through the sunlit day, right through the silent watches of the night. Sincerity and austerity characterise the band of faith-inspired men who make these ever-constant intercessions. And, as one of our correspondents wrote last week, they teach a lesson. The material aspect of the trouble has been magnified out of all proportion to the facts. The claim that the public from the mainland are entitled to the unrestricted use of certain parts of the Island, that they can land and roam at will over them, is untenable. When Caldey was purchased by the present owners there went with it those rights and privileges which have been in existence for generations. But though the Community have complete jurisdiction over the Island, they do not at the same time make it a 'close preserve'. They recognise that Caldey possesses features of great interest to the outside public, and welcomes visitors, provided—and this is the whole crux of the matter—they observe certain restrictions on their movements. The Community refuse to admit that outsiders can come and go at will. They contend they have a legal right to impose rules and regulations, the observance of which is a condition of entry to the Island. Those who see fit to dispute this claim are only stirring up unnecessary trouble. They might just as well maintain that they have a right to roam at large over the private domain of a landed proprietor. The contention that the road from the Jetty to the Lighthouse is a public thoroughfare has no foundation in fact. It is just as private as any other part of the Island. The only people who are entitled to use it freely are officials from Trinity House. Sunday 'landing parties', bent on demonstrating the 'rights of British subjects' may be spectacular and dramatic, but if persisted in all they are likely to achieve is the starting of an action at law, in which it is not unlikely the participants in these buccaneering expeditions would be the sufferers. Caldey is essentially an 'Isle of Peace', and it is a pity there should be found people not only willing but anxious to stir up strife and impose it as a substitute for that harmony and concord which from time immemorial have reigned there unchallenged until today.

Those who know Tenby will easily visualise Br Thomas pushing his head round the door of the Editor's office and, with a smile on his face, putting him in the picture about what was really happening. Meanwhile, wonderful public relations officer that he was, he had talked to the boatmen and sorted out their problems.

Earlier in 1936, Sir Reginald Clarry, M.P. for Newport, and Chairman of the Welsh Parliamentary Party, had taken the matter up with Walter Runciman, President of the Board of Trade. Towards the end of November he wrote to the *Western Mail* and, referring to the controversy to which they had given much prominence, said that he had been making a number of enquiries and had also been in close touch with the Home Office.

'It may interest your readers', he wrote, 'to know that the freehold of practically the whole of the Island above high-water mark is vested in three ecclesiastics, who are all British subjects. These gentlemen hold the property upon trust for a Community of Cistercians.'

The remainder of the letter merely stated what had long since been recognised and accepted by people of commonsense and goodwill. It also made it evident that there was no need for any animosity if it were not deliberately fomented by mischievous people. It is interesting to note that on this occasion there was no abbreviation owing to 'considerations of space'.

The attentions of the police, chiefly because of Mrs King's activities, were a constant worry to the Community at this time. The Journal's brief entry for February 22nd, 1935, had been:

Departure of Br Bartholomew for Citeaux. This caused some difficulties with the police, always very demanding for information! Where? When? and Why? this departure.

Such entries contrast oddly with some of the others.

1930
June 15th. Feast of the Holy Trinity. Some warships, submarines and destroyers anchored near Paul Jones Bay. Twenty Catholics, of whom three were Captains, assisted at the High Mass. After the

Mass Fr Daniel addressed them, then all sang 'Faith of Our Fathers' and 'God save the King.' Later they visited the monastery. That afternoon a dozen religious were invited to visit one of the submarines where all were served with tea.

(Fortunately no intrepid *Western Mail* reporter had unearthed the deadly secret of those, whose sacred trust was the defence of the realm, who had consorted in this way with these undesirable and highly suspect aliens!)

1932

April 11th. Br Anselm returned to France for his military service.
Sept 19th. Departure of Br Nivard for military service in Belgium.
Nov 13th. Extras served at dinner in honour of Br Bartholomew who has been awarded the Military Medal by the French Government.

1933

May 6th. Visit of Monsieur Sol, French Consul at Cardiff, who came to the Abbey in order to present Br Bartholomew (Corporal Arthur Colonet) with the Military Medal. After a short speech of welcome by the Prior, before the whole Community, the Consul replied, read the citation and pinned the medal on Br Bartholomew, giving him the accolade to the applause of all present.

1935

May 6th. 25th Anniversary of King George V accession to the throne. Union Jacks fly everywhere on the Island. Great celebrations including illuminations.

1936

July 7th. Fr Abbot urged upon all to become as English as possible using every means to live according to the customs and ways of their adopted country.

By this time there was considerable unrest in Europe and much talk of spies. It so happened that, in that same year, 1936, a frequent visitor to Caldey, Geoffrey Hoare, published a book called *Caldey, Isle of the Severn Sea*. It was an innocuous enough publication, but it contained a highly fanciful story of a German submarine putting two German naval officers ashore on Caldey during the First World War, and of one of them putting some flowers on the grave of one of the Benedictine monks. Harmless though the story was, it was of no help to the monks just then. To this day there are people who have a vague idea of having heard that Caldey was used by spies in touch with submarines off-shore during the 1914-18 war, forgetting (if they ever knew) that the present Order of 'foreigners' did not come until long afterwards.

In the early 1970's, when I had started research for this book, I well remember telling a fellow journalist, the late and highly respected John Winter of the *Daily Mail*, what I was working on, and he told me to be sure to find out if I could about the Caldey connection with submarines and spies during the First World War. He didn't know any details, he said, but remembered vaguely having heard something about it.

By the following summer, 1937, Mrs King seemed to have forgotten something of her previously expressed aversion to foreigners and had 'cultivated' Emperor Haile Selassie of Ethiopia, who was then in exile. Mrs King invited four of the children of his family to spend the summer months on Caldey with her own two little girls with whom they were in school near Bath. The details supplied to the press by Mrs King were that 'the young visitors included Prince Sahle Selassie (younger son of the Emperor Haile Selassie), Princesses Route and Sabil, and little Prince Iskundra (youngest son of the late Ras Desta).'

Mrs King also let it be known that she was arranging for the Emperor and some of his entourage to stay on Caldey but, unfortunately, she had not deemed it necessary to consult with the Prior beforehand. Permission was refused, mainly because the monks had no facilities for receiving such a party and, in any case, would not have wished to become unnecessarily involved in something which had political implications. Mrs King was, of course, highly displeased. Not surprisingly, and indeed perhaps inevitably, the monastery Journal's entry for October 23rd, 1937, reads, 'Another enquiry by the police to examine the foreign members of the Community and the foreign visitors (relations or friends) who visit the Island.'

Mrs King died suddenly in 1948 in the Island's village hall, immediately after the end of a play she had put on as part of the twenty-first birthday celebrations of Jerry Cummins, a member of an Island family with close connections with the monastery. Her husband then claimed the rights to the house. He was a quiet, inoffensive man in poor health, and the monks had no desire to dispute anything with him, but when he died four years later they made it clear that there were to be no more family claims upon the house.

Such was the background to much of the animosity directed against the monks in their earlier years on Caldey. And, as Fr Pascal said with a gentle smile, 'We all have our weaknesses.'

7
HOW THEY FARED IN SPITE OF IT

*'Therefore, brethren, stand fast, and hold
the traditions which ye have been taught'*:
2. Thessalonians 2:15

Whilst the monks in these first critical years in their new
home were facing up, albeit bewildered and uncomprehending,
to the troubles being deliberately created for them by others,
and struggling to maintain themselves on the production from
their Island farm, at a time when even some of the strongest
and oldest established of farmers were going to the wall
financially, they still had to remember, and give priority to,
their monastic vocation. And even here they had problems.

Obviously, the effect of these external problems would have
impinged upon the silence of the cloister and life within the
monastery walls, but here, too, there were still more difficulties
peculiar to the new foundation. Fundamentally, it was a
problem of language. Reference has already been made to the
obvious delight with which the profession of Br Thomas was
received as being the first by an English novice, as if to say they
were really in business at last. And by that time they had been
on Caldey almost six years. During those years a number of
English-speaking novices had joined the Community but, for
various reasons, had left it.

To survive, it was necessary for the Community to settle
down in the area and be accepted by their mainland neighbours
for purposes of trade. And to do this, it was essential for them
to learn the language. Fortunately for them, Tenby was very
much in the English-speaking area known as Little England
Beyond Wales. Even so, what must have been the difficulties
for the monks who, at that time, maintained a considerable
degree of silence, and who therefore had little opportunity to
practise by conversing, added to the fact that their commitments to prayer and toil left little time for learning a new
language? Whatever those difficulties must have been, they
had to be overcome for, as Br Thomas said in what reads as a

cry from the heart in a long letter to Bishop Vaughan of
Menevia during the trouble being made for them in 1936, 'The
aim of the foundation was, and is, to foster English vocations
to the Cistercian life and become an entirely British Community.'

Apart from the spiritual aims of the Community there was,
too, the need for an increase in the numbers to cope with the
physical labour involved in living on an island. Land, and farm
buildings, needed a great deal of work on them before they
could be brought to the high standard which the Cistercians set
themselves. There was also the work in the garden. Then,
again, and it is a point not readily appreciated by the mainland
dweller, anything delivered to Caldey would only be delivered
to the landing slip, and not to the monastery itself. And this
included the coal needed by the Community and the Islanders.
Before the coming of mains electricity in 1965 these needs were
considerable.

The coal was delivered by ketch, and this would be beached
in Prior Bay so that the horses and carts could be driven down
to it to unload. The coal was then carted up to the storage place
and tipped. For the monks, it meant hard work, with every
physically fit member of the Community doing his part in the
common cause. Time was the enemy, and no-one, on these
occasions, would need reminding that time, and particularly
tide, waited for no man as they sweated to complete their dirty
task before thc vessel was again afloat. Shifting more than a
hundred tons of coal between tides was an event of moment on
Caldey, and one of the least exciting and soul-inspiring aspects
of a monk's calling.

In the spring of their first year on Caldey the monks received
a visit from Dr Vaughan, Bishop of Menevia. Dom Anselm Le
Bail, Abbot of Chimay, was on the Island at the time and, in his
address of welcome to 'Cistercian Caldey', having said that St
Stephen Harding, an Englishman, had claimed that Cistercians
loved both the site (Citeaux) and the Rule, and that their
twelfth century predecessors had loved the land of Britain,
taking the language and customs of the Welsh, he then went on
to say:

> So we can speak today at Caldey, coming as we have from Belgium.
> We also are loving the land of Caldey and loving the Rule. Before

long we will love as well the land of Wales and the See of Menevia. So today in consequence we ought to work for the Kingdom of Christ in that country.

In his reply, Bishop Vaughan said:

> I sincerely wish you the greatest success. May you have a large and flourishing English-speaking novitiate in the near future. By your gallant self-sacrifice and prayer you will render aid in the finest manner for the conversion of England.

This reference to the aim of conversion is worth noting, and will perhaps be seen to have significance later on, when a look is taken at what has been happening on Caldey in more recent years.

On their arrival at Caldey a few months before the Bishop's visit, the monks had received a number of greetings. One of these had come from Cardinal Bourne, Archbishop of Westminster, and in it he had said, 'I beg God to bless you, and all your Community, and to enable you by the fervour of your earnest lives to give Him great honour and glory and thus bring about the salvation of many souls.'

He said nothing about the conversion of a whole nation.

So the monks stuck to their task, and by 1934 they had warranted being given a measure of autonomy, to the extent that they were allowed to elect their own Prior, whereas for the first five years he had been appointed by Chimay. Amidst all the problems and outside pressures they prayed and toiled through the ten difficult years which led up to the Second World War—an event of considerable significance to these Belgians and Frenchmen, so far from their native lands and families.

The Journal for these ten years includes much detail of arrivals and departures, clothing of novices, professions and ordinations. Much of it would be of little interest in a work such as this. On the other hand, when we remember particularly the close consideration which has already been given to different aspects of the monks' life, and their difficulties in wresting a living from an island farm, some of the entries, in addition to those already quoted in the previous chapter, are more than sufficient to tell their own story of what was happening on

Caldey and what life on the Island must have entailed. Entries previously referred to are included briefly in brackets.

1929

Feb 8th. Departures for Chimay of Rev Fr Abbot—he intends to return for Easter with other monks for Caldey.

Feb 28th. Death of the Rev Abbot General Dom Jean Baptiste Ollitrault de Keryvallan. This was the man responsible for keeping Caldey for the monastic life, first as a great friend and adviser to the Benedictines from the time of their conversion, and later for handling the transactions that led to the purchase of the Island, and the installation of his own children.

Apr 20th. First visit of Mgr Vaughan, Bishop of Menevia, to the new Community. Solemn reception by procession from the hall to the Abbey Church where the Te Deum was sung. The Abbot welcomed the Bishop and offered the devotion of the monks in his apostolate in Wales.

Tea was taken in the guest-house.

May 30th. Feast of Corpus Christi. According to established custom at Caldey, there would be a procession in the village after vespers. Three altars were erected, one at St Philomena's, the second at the Old Priory, and the third in the tea garden. Unfortunately the bad weather prevented the people from Tenby and Pembroke (with their parish priests) taking part.

June 5th. Foundation of the Novitiate.

Today Fr Abbot arrived with a group from Chimay to set up the new novitiate. It was composed of Fr Aelred Lefevre, the novice master, three novices, Fr Jean-Baptiste (priest and later Fr Illtyd), Br Alois (later Samson), Br Victor (later Benedict), and a postulant who will take the name of Paul. Br David, our own postulant, will be added to give a total of six. This group, including the Fr Master, had left Chimay much as the main body had done in solemn procession, and also carrying a Foundation Cross, and in addition a copy of the Rule of St Benedict with commentaries given by Dom Anselm to the novices at Chimay. On arrival at Caldey they had taken up the procession again and were received by the Community, thence to the church for the singing of the Te Deum. After this all proceeded again solemnly to the apartment set aside for the new novitiate. Tea was taken by all in the guest-house. On the 7th June Fr Abbot declared the novitiate canonically established and gave the habit to the two new postulants.

July 25th. On this day, due to the generosity and kindness of the Prior and Community of Prinknash, the relic of St Samson was brought back to Caldey and given to the Cistercian Community. It was carried by Dom Columba from Prinknash. It is interesting to note that it was the late Abbot General of the Cistercians who had originally obtained this relic of the early monk of Caldey, Samson, who later became the Bishop of Dol in Brittany.

July 26th. Arrival of Dom Anselm accompanied by Mgr Leroy, Principal of the College of Chimay, Rev Fr Alphonse Bernigaud, Dom Léon Ehard, Abbot of Tre Fontane, our monastery in Rome, and Dom John Daly, Definitor from Rome.

July 28th. All the above had come to celebrate the Feast of St Samson, Celtic monk and Patron of the Island. All assisted at Pontifical High Mass, but unhappily rain prevented the procession planned.

July 29th. The following day (Monday) was fixed for the Islanders' celebration. In the morning an exhibition of needle-work and garden produce. The workmen from the monastery had a special lunch in the guest-house. In the afternoon several sporting competitions, and finally a social evening in the hall given by the Islanders, which was attended by the Superiors and monastery guests. For the Religious there was rest from manual work and permission was given to relax the monastic silence.

Aug 17th. Departure for Mount St Bernard's of our first English novice, Br Bernard Hyde.

[Sept 27th. The fire on the Caldey boat—the Teresina.]

Sept 29th. Dom Alberic Styles, O.S.B., of Prinknash, a native of Caldey (where his family still live), and member of the old Benedictine Community here, arrived to celebrate his first Mass at the monastery.

Oct 23rd. First regular visitation of Caldey. This was made by Dom Bonaventure de Groote of Notre Dame de Sainte- Sixte, the Mother House of Chimay, since Caldey was still indeed a part of the Notre Dame de Scourmont Community. The record says that in spite of his distaste for sea trips he decided to visit the young foundation.

Dec 25th. Christmas! According to custom established at Caldey the Islanders were invited to the *reveillon* after the midnight Mass in the guest-house.

1930

Jan 7th. During the night (6/7) first anniversary of the foundation, Br Alberic (lay-brother) died. He was discovered on his bed as though sleeping. It was especially moving as he had intended to return to Notre Dame de Westmalle the next day and had bade goodbye to many on the Island. He was one of the early advance party and had come to Caldey in July 1928.

Jan 25th. Re-opening of the village and parish church of St David's after repairs. From now on the Islanders could have their own services there. Fr Patrick Rafferty would attend to the parish duties.

Feb 28th. Installation of new washing machine in the laundry and also a drying machine, both bought second-hand, the original items having been collected by the Benedictine Community, as also the mahogany tables from the refectory. The bells, however, still remain in the tower.

May 30th. Unexpected arrival of Dom Anselm. As Fr Rémy (now back at Chimay) had been in charge of the archives and records, Fr Bertin was now appointed to take on this responsibility together with the accounting.

June 20th. Arrival of Most Rev Fr Abbot General Dom Hermann Smets. He was accompanied by Dom Anselm, Dom Etienne (Definitor) and Fr Charles Perpete, Chaplain to the Cistercian nuns of Chimay. A solemn reception and procession was organised, the Te Deum sung and the Rev Abbot General addressed the Community in the Chapter House, telling them how happy he was to be with the 'Benjamins' of the Order.

[June 24. Everyone at the haymaking under the direction of the Abbot!]

June 29th. Dom Anselm preached on the necessity for calm, patience and unity in the new Community.

July 24th. The Abbot of Chimay returned with four monks to reinforce the Community—Fr Gall and Fr Jean-Baptiste to replace Br Illtyd and Br Samson returning for military service. Fr Jerome and Fr Albert also came but were to remain only two months— both were Chimay students in Rome.

July 29th. Fr Prior and Superior Dom Andrew Garcette, announced his definite departure for Belgium as he was being recalled for other tasks. His departure was regretted by all, Community and Islanders.

Fr Aelred Lefevre was appointed as the new Superior.

July 31st. Fr Basil, the cellarer, and Fr Bertin, the accountant, went to Swansea to set up arrangements (book-keeping, etc.) with a chartered accountant.

Sept 7th. Fr Basil and Fr Hyacinth went to Neath to take part in the celebration of 8th Centenary of the Foundation of Neath (Cistercian) Abbey (1130). The High Mass would be celebrated by Dom Celsus O'Connell, Abbot of Mount St Bernard's, and Fr Basil and Fr Hyacinth were to be deacon and sub-deacon. The latter shaved off his beautiful beard which he had kept as a souvenir of his days in Japan.

[Sept 27th. Afternoon—the last sheaves of oats were brought in and threshed.]

Nov 15th. Visit of Dom Anselm. He spoke of the Abbey of Chimay and how great was the intake of lay-brothers.

Nov 26th. Dom Anselm concerned himself with making rules for the study of English and at the same time keeping the normal rule of silence in view. He had accepted Fr Basil's request for a few months rest and spiritual retreat. Fr Charles would carry on as cellarer.

1931

Jan 20th. Br David (novice) operated on for appendicitis at Tenby Hospital.

Feb 2nd. Fr Basil now very tired, returned to Chimay for a time—impossible for him to find tranquillity at Caldey.

Apr 6th. Simple profession of Br Andrew. Fr Prior speaking of the day's liturgy about God delivering the Jews from the bondage and slavery of Egypt and making them a people consecrated to himself. He likened this choice and consecration to the monastic life.

This evening the Prior blessed a cross of stone, gift [?] of Major O'Neill, to take the place of the small wooden one we had on the wall of the Abbey Church.

Apr 23rd. Arrival of Br Hippolyte and Br Stanislaus—lay-brother novices from Chimay—sent to replace Br Joseph of Rochefort for the kitchen, cooking etc.

Apr 27th. Visit of Mgr Vaughan, Bishop of Menevia. He spoke to the Community assembled in the chapter of his confidence in the power of prayer, of contemplation, of silence, and of the presence of God.

Apr 28th. At 8 a.m. the Bishop invited the Community to assist in his Mass celebrated at the Church of St Illtyd (the Old Priory). The office of Terce was sung there and it was, of course, the first time we had sung the Divine Office in this old monastic sanctuary of the pre-Reformation days.

May 21st. The carillon belonging to the Benedictines is finally taken down and despatched to Prinknash.

July 16th. Feast of St Stephen Harding. Simple profession of Br David, Br Anselm and Br Jean-Baptiste, all from Chimay, and Fr Prior reminded the Community that so far none of the English postulants had remained.

July 28th. Feast of St Samson—Patron of Caldey. The prior of Prinknash assisted at the Island celebrations and procession. The Rev Ivor Daniel, parish priest of Pembroke Dock, and the Rev P. Moran, parish priest of Tenby, came with some of their parishioners.

Aug 30th. The Rev Canon Chavez from Brittany (France) came to Caldey on pilgrimage and preached to the Community on the part played in the evangelisation of his country by St Paul de Léon, a disciple of St Illtyd and St Samson of Caldey.

Nov 1st. Report by Dom Anselm on his visits to our monasteries in Ireland—Melleray and Roscrea. Both were flourishing with many vocations. Schools attached were successful, also materially a good report. Life there very disciplined and strict. Enclosures very well kept.

1932

Jan 1st. Return of Fr Basil after almost a year of rest at Chimay.

Jan 7th. Postulant lay-brother received—Mr Patrick Moore.

Mar 6th. Visit of Dom Anselm. At the Chapter the Abbot explained that the foundation would now be given a certain amount of autonomous administration, and he invited a discussion by the Community.

Mar 13th. At the Chapter Rev Fr Abbot gave to Fr Prior and Superior certain powers of administration.

Apr 19th. First Community retreat preached in English. Preached by Fr Joseph, Passionist from Carmarthen. It was especially for the English members and the French found it a great trial.

June 5th. Frederick Jenkins and Gerard Troes, both familiars, rescued after being caught by the tide while visiting the Cathedral caves. Br Christopher and the Islanders saved them from a serious and dangerous situation by boat.

Sept 1st. Incognito visit of a reporter from the Cardiff *Western Mail*. He took his information only from the Islanders and then prepared a series of articles on Caldey entitled, 'The most mysterious island in Britain.' He attempted to show (1) that there was conflict between the Community and the world outside, and (2) that a sort of mystery was being jealously kept on Caldey.

However, replies, just as scathing, were made by Fr Ivor Daniel of Pembroke Dock, and Mr Diamond, Editor of the *Catholic Herald*.

Sept 4th. Blessing of the large Cross overlooking the quay. The figure of Christ is the gift of Mrs Roch and the work (sculpture in wood) was done by Mr Mahoney of Messrs Burns, Oates and Washbourne of London.

Sept 14th. Clothing of Br Thomas (the postulant Mr Patrick Moore). The sermon on the occasion was preached by his uncle.

1933

Jan 6th. Anniversary of the foundation. Exhibition of photographs and cuttings from newspapers in cloisters. However, being a Friday, dinner was most austere.

Feb 6th. Visit of Dom Anselm and Fr Sebastian, the accountant of Chimay.

Feb 17th. Fr Sebastian, accountant of Chimay, and Fr Bertin, accountant of Caldey, went to London to consult with Mgr Cardon de Wiart on question of accountancy.

[Feb 24th. Heavy snow, telephone off and boat failing to start.]

[May 6th. Br Bartholomew receives Military Medal.]

June 18th. As it was hoped that the Community of Caldey might be granted autonomy at the next General Chapter in September, Rev Fr Prior put it to the founders that they might wish to return to Chimay for some weeks before making a vow of Stability to Caldey.

July 12th. Arrival of Dom Simon of Notre Dame de Tilbourg delegated to make the regular visitation. He was accompanied by Dom Anselm and Br Francis de Giraudot, solemnly professed monk of Chimay, who hoped to remain at Caldey.

July 24th. Examination of three questions in view of the monastery becoming autonomous:-

(1) Is there a possibility of electing from the Community a titular Prior?

(2) Are there likely to be novices?

(3) Is the future (material) of the Abbey sure?

Aug 29th. Visit of Mr and Mrs Collins, Mayor of Tenby.

Sept 8th. Blessing of the statue of Our Lady donated by the family Cardon de Lichtbuer (Fr Dominic). It was placed in the garden of enclosure.

Sept 18th. Telegram from Citeaux granting autonomy to Caldey Abbey.

Sept 30th. 1.30 p.m. Extraordinary meeting of the Community to hear more details of the autonomous future of Caldey.

3.30. p.m. Arrival of Dom Anselm, Fr Dominic (who had been to Chimay for some weeks), and two young priests of the Mother House who hoped to remain at Caldey, Fr Peter and Fr Herman.

Nov 1st. Feast of All Saints. At Chapter the Abbot explained the reason for his visit, i.e. to decide which members would form the future Community, and to this end each monk should go to the Abbot with his opinion and decision.

Nov 6th. At Chapter the Abbot read (in Latin, French and English) the official request to Rome requesting autonomy for the Abbey. This had to be signed by each member of the Community who wished to form part of the new monastery.

Nov 9th. The question of learning English again arises for a silent Order (i.e. within the enclosure). It is now thought that listening to the radio at times of talks, etc., might greatly assist.

Dec 3rd. Profession of Br Bartholomew. Fr Prior spoke of the desire and demand of the monk for union with God, but the necessity of the desire and demand for the Cross, by which alone could man release himself from selfishness in order to be united to God.

1934

Jan 11th. The Rev Fr Aelred Lefevre was elected by the votes of the solemnly professed monks to be the first titular Prior of the monastery of Caldey.

Jan 14th. High Mass celebrated by Dom Godefroid (now Auxiliary Abbot of Citeaux) in thanksgiving for the Caldey events of past few days. Dom Aelred officially installed as Superior in the Chapter where he received the keys and the seal of the monastery. All the professed monks, each in turn, promised obedience to the new Superior. The newly elected Prior was then conducted to the stall in the choir which he would occupy. The Te Deum was sung.

Apr 14th. The Bishop of Menevia (Mgr Vaughan) addressed the Community during the evening in the Chapter house. He spoke of his happiness in being at Caldey and how much he counted on their life of prayer and sacrifice for the good of his Diocese. He told the monks that at a recent audience with the Pope in Rome, His Holiness had stressed that the conversion to Christ would come to Wales (as elsewhere) by prayer and sacrifice.

June 18th. In order to be ready to discharge a cargo of coal, a team of monks retired to bed at 8 p.m. Rose at midnight, said private Mass, took breakfast and began work at once in order to finish unloading while the tide was low and before the boat floated again.

July 16th. Solemn profession of Br David. The preacher, a Benedictine monk of St André, developed the theme that God has loved us and we must return this love with love by first keeping the commandments and the evangelical counsels.

July 26th. Arrival of Dom Anselm who, when giving a report on conditions, etc., at Chimay, told us they had started to distribute soup daily at the monastery door to the poor and unemployed— between twenty and forty daily.

Aug 19th. Fr Francis and Fr Benedict ordained priests by Mgr Vaughan, Bishop of Menevia. The Bishop, preaching, likened the contemplative life to the work behind the tapestry—hidden but essential to the beauty of the work shown on the other side.

Sept 12th. Harvest completed—thanks be to God not as bad as anticipated after the extremely dry June and the storms of August.

[Sept 29th. At last! The first profession of an English novice—Br Thomas.]

1935

Feb 20th. Sealed post bag fell in the sea, and the letters arrived all soaked.

[Departure of Br Bartholomew. Difficulties with the police.]

Mar 15th. Rev Fr Prior and Fr Patrick to Wrexham for Requiem for Mgr Vaughan, our Bishop.

[May 6th. King George V Silver Jubilee.]

July 8th. Cargo of 20,000 bricks for the construction of new electricity station. Discharged in two periods from 2 p.m. to 7.30 p.m. on the 8th and between 5 a.m. and 8 a.m. on the 9th. Very hard work!

Sept 25th. Fr Prior and Fr Patrick for Wrexham for consecration of Dr Michael McGrath, new Bishop of Menevia.

Oct 27th. Fr Odo the Sub-Prior requested to be relieved of his post as Cellarer. Fr Prior decided to divide the work into three sections—Fr Jerome, interior of monastery, and the needs of the monks—Br Christopher, the farm—and Br Thomas, the boat and all the liaison with business outside.

1936

Feb 11th. For several days a great cold east wind has blown across the Island. Great deal of damage and trees uprooted.

May 17th. Blessing of the Sacred Heart statue now placed in the cloister garth facing the main door.

June 11th. 125 people came from Tenby, Pembroke Dock and Haverfordwest with their parish priests to celebrate the Feast of Corpus Christi.

July 2nd. Regular visitation by Rev Fr Abbot of Chimay. Discussion and examination on the distressing question of the recruitment of novices.

Lecture on the discipline of liturgical prayer in order to produce atmosphere of absolute peace in choir.

July 3rd. Lecture on the necessity of Lectio Divina, especially for those with much work to do. Free time should thus be devoted to spiritual reading in order to stimulate mind and spirit.

July 4th. Lecture on Manual Work.

This is a necessary part of our life. However, it is also necessary to see that for most of the Community it does not go beyond the hours laid down by the Rule. Care must be taken that the lay brothers have the opportunity to attend the Chapter and be present for the readings. Initiative should be allowed to those in charge of various offices.

July 5th. Dom Anselm spoke of the common joy and peace absolutely necessary for the spiritual life of the monk living in Community.

July 6th. The characteristics of the Cistercians were especially a well-kept enclosure and attention to the silence necessary for recollection. Our life was worship by the Divine Office, study and manual work. Remember always it is not the exact observance of the less important rules that is a sign of sanctity.

[July 7th. Finally Fr Abbot urged upon all to become as English as possible using every means to live according to the customs and ways of their adopted country.]

July 27th. Wedding at parish church—'Willie' Styles.

[Aug 21st. Visit of chief of police.]

[Sept 8th. Tenby refuses Caldey tomatoes.]

1937

May 29th. 'Si vis pacem, para bellum'—for several days an aircraft has been passing over Caldey trailing a long red cloth. It is said to be for anti-aircraft shooting practice.

June 13th. Arrival of Mgr McGrath, Bishop of Menevia, to confirm minor orders on Br Anselm. This was the first visit of the new Bishop. Arrival also of Dom Celsus, Abbot of Mount Melleray (Ireland).

July 23rd. Talk given by Mgr R. R. Knox. He exhorted the Community to pray for Spain, caught up in a Civil War.

July 28th. The children and grandchildren of the Emperor of Ethiopia are to be seen in the garden of Mrs King's house.

Aug 19th. Arrival of Dom Anselm for the regular visitation.

Aug 20th. Feast of St Bernard, and the Abbot took the opportunity to urge the Community to study well the life of this Cistercian Father, his doctrine and his example.

Sept 6th. Visit of Fr Prior to the Benedictines at Prinknash.

[Oct 23rd. Another enquiry by police.]

Nov 14th. Only ten choir monks for the office of Matins, but this night office sung as usual.

Installation of new stove (Esse) in the kitchen—will use anthracite which is easy to obtain at Saundersfoot.

1938

Jan 7th. Mr McHardy very ill and taken to Tenby hospital. Later, thanks to the generosity of Mrs Roch, he was taken to Abergavenny.

Jan 15th. Bad storm and the sub-marine telephone line which links Caldey to Tenby by Giltar Point is broken.

Jan 22nd. Some monks and Islanders returning from Tenby were enveloped in thick fog and direction was lost. After three quarters of an hour they found themselves near to the rocks off Penally.

Mar 21st. Fr Denys Warrington, the accountant of Mount St Bernard's, Leicester, has obtained for us certain tax relief in relation to the solemnly professed monks.

The old 'look-out' or 'watch-hut' near the lighthouse has been replaced by the Board of Trade by a modern set-up.

May 17th. Fr Prior attended the Jubilee celebrations of Fr Ivor Daniel (25 years' priesthood) at Pembroke Dock. He had rendered many services to the Community since their arrival in 1928.

May 27th. The authorities at Tenby have insisted upon three members of the Community and one Islander attending a civil defence course in the event of war. The course to cover emergencies such as gas attack, incendiary bombing, bombardment, etc.

Br Thomas (English), Fr Dominic (Belgian), Fr Pascal (French), and Mr South made up the team.

Sept 26th. Return of Fr Prior from the General Chapter at Citeaux. Fr Odo, Sub-Prior, had a stroke and his right side more or less paralysed.

Sept 29th. International situation reference Czechoslovakia is very strained. An agreement has been made between Hitler and Mussolini, on the one part, and Chamberlain and Daladier on the other. Situation is calmer. Fr Herman is mobilised and has to report to Belgium.

Oct 24th. 25th anniversary of the Abbatial Blessing of Dom Anselm Le Bail, Abbot of Notre Dame de Scourmont and Fr Immediate of Notre Dame de Caldey.

Nov 25th. After a violent storm a great deal of new wood was washed up at Sand Top Bay and after an inspection by the Receiver of Wrecks we bought this lot very cheaply.

1939

Feb 14th. Requiem Mass for Pope Pius XI. Caldey has a special reason to pray for him since he had requested that the Island should become a Cistercian property in the first instance.

Mar 2nd. Cardinal Pacelli elected Pope. (Pius XII).

Mar 26th. Gas masks tried on.

June 8th. Usual procession of Corpus Christi. In spite of rough seas, many visitors.

June 10th. Arrival of Bishop McGrath to confer sub-diaconate on Br Anselm. Talking to the Community he told them to be very thankful for their vocation and that they played an important role in Society.

June 14th. Visit of the Lord Mayor of Cardiff and the Mayor of Tenby. 'The party very much enjoyed their experience on the island' reported the *Tenby Observer*.

June 29th. Br Christopher received the Last Sacraments.

July 6th. Arrival of Dom Anselm.

July 7th. Fr Basil, Cellarer from 1928 to 1934, during which time he became very exhausted, requests a return to Chimay for an indefinite period.

July 10th—13th. The Abbot gives instructions in case of war. The consuls will call for those to be mobilised. Administration of the Community in the case of the Superior's departure, in case of expulsion or evacuation.

July 18th. Death of Br Christopher. At 3 p.m. all were called together to assist at the bedside and recite the prayers for the dying. 5 p.m. he moved towards death, quiet and peaceful, and finally slept in the Lord.

July 23rd. Fr Prior spoke about the life and character of this quite remarkable Brother (Christopher) who had played such a part in the establishment of their Community at Caldey.

July 31st. International situation more and more tense. Many precautionary measures have to be taken—black out windows, prepare underground shelter, etc.

Throughout these entries it is possible to see, not only the Community's concern for their spiritual needs and the problems facing them, but a clear pattern in which they were steadily cementing their ties of friendship with the Islanders, and also the mainland, both in sickness and in health, in their joys and in their sorrows.

Quite obviously, the Journal was written up sporadically, which will account, not only for a slight change of tense in some cases, but for the fact that an entry recording the arrival of two new brothers could, at the same time, anticipate their departures two months later. It will also account for the occasional phrase 'the record says', and gives added significance to the question mark immediately after the reference to the 'gift' in the entry concerning O'Neill's cross. The correspondence about him shows that he left the Island very shortly afterwards and that the Community already had good grounds for believing that they would probably have to pay for the gift themselves.

It is perhaps odd to find the term Abbey being used in reference to Caldey when they achieved a degree of autonomy in 1933, because they remained a Priory and did not become an Abbey in their own right until much later. It is also worth noting that, although Fr Aelred Lefevre had been Prior up till that time, he had been appointed in that capacity by the mother house at Chimay, and it did not necessarily follow that he would now be elected by the Community, as will be seen when later reference is made to the time when Caldey did eventually become established as an Abbey in its own right. Caldey, of course, had been an Abbey in the time of the Benedictines and the title tended to persist.

One other reference which will be of particular interest, to local people at any rate, is the one which concerns anthracite coal being readily available at Saundersfoot. The Bonville's Court Colliery, with its world-famous anthracite, at Saundersfoot, had closed in 1930. This coal had been shipped from Saundersfoot harbour for many years. For a short time after the closure of Bonville's Court, desultory attempts were being made to maintain an industry which had contributed much to the area in the past but which was now virtually dead. In 1937 anthracite was being mined again at Stepaside and being driven by lorries to Saundersfoot, because the romantic little railway line which had served the pits in the area had already reached the final stages before, at last, being abandoned.

But how many islanders, it is permissible to wonder, are on record as having called in the Receiver of Wrecks to pay him for what those who dwell in lonely places by the sea have traditionally regarded as their birthright?

And so the Journal helps to bring the story to the time when the dark clouds, which for long had been gathering over Europe, burst at last into the threatened storm. The family of monks on Caldey knew as much about it as most families. The sorrow, the anxiety and hopes are all vividly evident in their Journal for the next six years. Some of their number had already been called up.

8
THE WAR YEARS

'And ye shall hear of wars and rumours of wars: see that ye be not troubled: for all these things must come to pass, but the end is not yet': Matthew 24:6

I can do no better than quote in some detail the relevant entries in the monastery Journal. These cover the years from September 1939 to January 1945, and portray a fascinating and revealing picture of the way in which a tight-knit religious Community faced the rigours and upheavals of a world war.

1939

Sept 2nd. Fr Prior understood from radio that all French personnel (class 1909-1924) should report to the Consulate General in London. Certain preparations were made.

Sept 3rd. Br Thomas made contact with Consul at Cardiff and was given to understand instructions had been sent.

Sept 4th. Post arrives. Orders for Frs Prior, Pascal, Edmund, Benedict, Anselm and Br Andrew to proceed to Southampton. By same post orders for Fr Herman to proceed to Brussels.

Sept 5th. 5 p.m. this evening the six monks named above proceeded to the little quay accompanied by the rest of the Community. At the little Chapel of Our Lady overlooking the sea everyone halted and sang the 'Salve Regina' commending the Community and their families to the protection of Our Lady. There remained at the monastery only 10 choir monks and 5 lay brothers.

Sept 10th. Radio message heard at supper in Polish and French calling on all Poles to enrol in the army.

Sept 13th. Letter from the Prior at Cherbourg. Here they wait (the Caldeyans) to be separated. He is anxious about Caldey.

Sept 14th. Instructions from Rev Fr Abbot of Scourmont giving some practical details for the Community. He has started a small bulletin *The Monk-Soldier* for the circulation among the Chimay/ Caldey mobilised. They think at Chimay that Fr Bertin has been called up—No! he still writes these records.

Sept 21st. Letters from Fr Prior dated the 15th. Daily communiqués from the *Daily Sketch* posted up.

Sept 23rd. Letter from Fr Benedict and card from Fr Edmund.

Sept 26th. Completed the potato harvest. Good harvest both in quantity and size. Final gathering in of fruit and honey—also both good harvests.

Oct 6th. Letter sent to each of our monks in the army with September news of Caldey.

Oct 9th. Letter from Fr Prior who is stretcher-bearer in his regiment. He has seen Fr Benedict who has already been demobilised and is living with his family near Cambrai.

Oct 10th. The son of the Secretary* of the British Legion at Tenby (English soldier) has met Fr Pascal in France (French soldier). The incident was related in the *Tenby Observer* and other English newspapers under the heading of, 'How small is the world'. 'Tenby man meets monk of Caldey in France'.

Oct 15th. It is established that mines are to be found at sea between Cardiff and Pembroke. An officer of the Coastguards has visited Caldey to suggest prudence if unidentified objects are found in or near the sea, and above all to keep a look-out and report any unusual things in and around the Island.

Oct 19th. For two weeks two or three postulants with a couple of monks have been trying to spread manure on one of the larger fields up near the lighthouse. Fr President is using the small tractor while the larger one is being used by one of the farm-hands. Fr Sub-Prior works on the park to try to clear the paths which have become overgrown.

Oct 25th. (1) News of Rev Fr Prior. He is in hospital at Cambrai with blood pressure and some stomach trouble.

(2) Fr Herman has been at Scourmont for three days and on the 15th was able to assist at the ordination of his brother Fr Desiré, monk of Chimay.

(3) Br Andrew is with the Engineers and helping to dig trenches. He says there is only one tap with water for washing between 400 men.

Nov 11th. Fr Prior remains in hospital but he hopes to be demobilised as those more than 40 years old are being sent home from the French Army. In this case he will probably return to Caldey. Fr Edmund writes that he has been moved. He is now quite close to the Junior Seminary of Reims and has very little to do.

Nov 14th. Fr Pascal finally joined up with his unit at Ancenis. After some tough nights without blankets he was offered the post of teacher of English at the local college. He gives eight hours each

*The English soldier referred to was Capt. A. D. Robins, Tenby.

week to the pupils of the second grade. He was able to lodge in the town and was billeted on an aged Countess. He occupies the 'Salon', and has three meals of meat every day, wine and muscatel. Supper every Sunday night with the Countess, often dinner with the Bishop, the Dean or other persons of rank!!

Nov 15th. Great activity around Caldey. One of four aircraft returning to base had crashed into the sea about a mile from Paul Jones Bay. Search carried out without success.

Nov 22nd. Letter from Fr Prior. He is demobilised and home with his family. He is making the necessary arrangements to return to Caldey.

Nov 23rd. Card from Fr Pascal who is also being demobilised and intends to return to Caldey instead of complying with a request of the Superior of the College to remain there for a few more weeks.

Nov 25th. Beetroot taken up. Work continues at least every afternoon.

Nov 26th. Interesting letter from Br Andrew but one suspects that he is finding the military life very hard in many ways.

Dec 6th. The Coastguards at Tenby report suspicious things going on in the Channel south of Caldey. Enemy submarine? They ask that we advise them immediately, day or night, if we see anything.

Dec 14th. Letter from Br Anselm. He is at Boulogne-sur-mer and it makes him dream of Caldey. He is more shoe-repairer than soldier.

Dec 16th. Received a photograph of Fr Edmund as sergeant— posted up on notice board. Also one of Br Andrew as soldier.

Dec 25th. Night office recited instead of sung, but the Christmas Mass at midnight solemnly sung. Lauds (morning prayer) also recited.

1940

Jan 9th. Letter read in the refectory from the Abbot General addressed to all monks serving with the Forces. Fr Prior reports that he hopes to be with us at the end of the week.

Jan 12th. Return of Fr Prior. All those monks free waited at the quay for his arrival and escorted him to the monastery guest-house. After dinner, dessert and coffee served there to welcome him until the time of manual work.

Many problems these days. Mr Rogers, the boatman, is ill and we have to find a stranger to help out. The sea is constantly rough. Worse, there is a cow in calf and the vet. is necessary. If we have to wait until tomorrow we may lose the cow.

Jan 13th. Arrival of the vet. finally this afternoon—calf delivered after 48 hours labour.

Jan 14th. Fr Prior spoke of his experiences in the army, then of the defence of France, Maginot Line, etc. Also of regulations for civilian shelters, blackouts, etc.

Jan 17th. Fr Edmund sends his wishes for Jan 1st. He has sung Mass for and addressed some English soldiers stationed near St Brice.

Fr Benedict, remobilised, is in Brittany and able to visit some Cistercian houses in that part.

Jan 19th. Br Anselm writes that things go well with him. He is billeted with a family and is able to play with the children. Letter from Fr Pascal. He is waiting to return to Caldey.

Jan 24th. Fr Pascal arrived this evening at 4 p.m.

Jan 25th. After dinner we had *café* in the guest-house in honour of the return of Fr Pascal.

Jan 26th. Fr Pascal gave a talk after the High Mass on his 'Campaign of Ancenis'.

Jan 27th. Letter from Br Anselm asking for cigarettes and English tea, etc. Letters from Fr Edmund and Fr Herman.

Feb 2nd. During the night a Norwegian vessel of 10,000 tons (Le Bel Pareil), making for Swansea for a cargo of coal, was off course in a thick fog and storm, and struck the rocks between Drinkim and Little Drinkim Bays. There was a crew of 32 men, many of whom are ill.

Feb 4th. Visit of the Insurance Agents to the 'Bel Pareil'. Mr Rogers, our boatman, taken ill with heart attack on the beach at Tenby, so there is an uncertainty about the boat service. Nearly all the Community down with 'flu.

Feb 5th. The fog remains very thick and it is impossible to signal by lamp with Tenby—it is necessary just to wait at the quay and watch for the boat.

Feb 8th. Card from Fr Edmund. He has spent a few days at Citeaux.

Feb 10th. Letter from Fr Herman. He has been at Notre Dame de Westmalle where he has met the Rev Fr Abbot General who is very tired and sad that so many monasteries are empty as a result of the general mobilisation.

Feb 12th. A group at Drinkim Bay is to take the fuel oil from the tank of the ship while another group try to take off the wood cargo.

Feb 15th. Further news of Fr Edmund from Citeaux. He writes that 46 monks are called up and 6 more expected. Only 35 lay brothers and 12 choir monks remain there. Dom Godefroid is very tired.

Feb 17th. In return for the services given to the Company of the Norwegian ship they offered us two lifeboats. The team of joiners working on the wreck were instructed to make a cabin for one and install an engine. The other could serve as a barge.

Feb 25th. Again instructions not to relax the rules of the 'black-out'.

Mar 3rd. 3 p.m. this afternoon all free to listen to the radio from Notre Dame de Paris. Lenten sermon by Mgr Chevrot.

Mar 10th. The authorities concerned with the wreck of the 'Bel Pareil' deplored particularly the absence of telephonic communication between Caldey and the mainland, and the question of the installation is raised again. During war-time there is therefore an absolute necessity and the various bodies responsible have taken the matter up again—Alas! The matter once again was forgotten with time!

Mar 22nd. Good Friday. So few in the Community that we did not sing the night office. After the office of Prime began the recitation of the Psalter—86 psalms were recited by two choirs.

Apr 17th. Finally after many attempts and failures two tugs from Swansea have managed to float the 'Bel Pareil' from Drinkim Bay round to Priory Bay. Great holes are now visible as the ship is up on the sand.

Apr 20th. This morning the Norwegian ship was floated in Priory Bay and left finally at 5.30 a.m. Towards 7.30 a.m. it could be seen like a cathedral flanked by two towers (the tugs) moving towards the Bristol Channel.

Apr 24th. The last choir novice leaves. The novitiate is empty.

May 10th. About 9 a.m. the Prior told us about the invasion of Holland and Belgium by the Germans and asked all the Belgians to be prepared for any eventuality. The following days watched with anxiety the progress of the invaders. Dinner was advanced in order that we might finish in time to hear the 12.30 news from 'Radio Paris'. The evenings at 6 p.m. we listened to London—the B.B.C. Home Service.

May 19th. The Prior assigned to every monk one hour of the day for special recollection and prayer. We have asked Canon Hope of Milford Haven (where Belgian refugees have arrived) to help in discovering if there are relations of the monks or any workers who would like to work on the farm. No news from Belgium or France since the invasion.

May 24th. We are following twice a day, on the radio, the events in France and Belgium. This evening, 'Empire Day', we heard the speech of H.M. King George VI, and the news that followed until

The founding monks leaving Chimay in Belgium, December 1928.

Passing through Cardiff on the way to Caldey. *Photo: Western Mail*

The 'Founding Fathers' on Caldey, January 6th, 1929. In the centre, Dom Anselm le Bail.

A visit by Dr. Vaughan, Bishop of Menevia, April 1929.

The first Novitiates, 5th June, 1929. Above before, and below after their reception.

A trip to the mainland, 1929.

Andre Garcette (left). The first Cistercian Prior of Caldey, together with Rev. Ivor Daniel, then priest at Pembroke Dock.

Removal of the bells from Caldey to Prinknash, 31st May, 1931.

The old Priory as it was in the 1930s.

The 'Stephen Harding', one of the early island boats, 1933.

Taking coal from the beached coal boat to the island store, *c.*1930.

Photo: Fox Photos

An early haymaking scene, *c.*1930.

Photo: Fox Photos

Brother Teilo fishing in the old Priory Fishpond, 1931.

The Community photographed on 14th January, 1934.

Reaping and binding in July 1934.

The island generator in about 1933.

The High Altar (later burnt) showing the Pre-Reformation stones sent
from other monasteries.

At work on the island in about 1935.

Unloading coal from the beach, *c*.1938.

Unloading coal from the beach, c.1938.

Tenby boatmen reading the Prior's notice restricting landing on Sunday and out of 'Season', August 24th, 1936.

Photo: Fox Photos

Timber washed up at Sandtop Bay, November 26th, 1938.

The first six monks to be called up on the outbreak of the war,
September 1939.

The Norwegian ship *'Belpareil'* aground at Little Drinkim Bay,
January 1940.

A visit from officers of the Belgian Army, August 1940.

9.30 p.m. The Prior intends to fix a set in the refectory so that we may hear the Belgian station during supper.

May 28th. After the High Mass Fr Prior announced the sad news of the capitulation by the King of the Belgians, Leopold III and his army. 12.30 we heard this news again on the radio from M. Paul Reynaud, Prime Minister of France. This evening we heard of the decision of the Belgian Government, now installed in Paris, to fight on. Same day we received word from Fr Charles, chaplain to the nuns of Chimay (Town). He says that on the 14th May two bombs fell on the chaplaincy. He has left with a train of evacuees—he is now a refugee in the Abbey Belle-Fontaine.

May 29th. As the postal service seems better we have sent a word to each of the Caldey monks on service to try to maintain contact. Fr Herman, however, a Belgian, will be more exposed and may be with those who capitulated—or evacuated with the ambulances?

May 30th. At dinner time we received a visit from some Belgian officers and men who are on rest at Tenby. The post brings more news from France and Belgium. The Rev Fr Abbot and Fr Gabriel have had to leave the Monastery of Scourmont. Fr Albert (Prior) has now been called up. Letter from Fr Edmund—he remains in the same place and often goes to Igny. There is some bombing and he has great fears for the monastery at Scourmont.

May 31st. Letter from Br Andrew describes how he escaped miraculously from the Boches during the retreat. First day a march of 50 kilometres with all equipment on his back. Second day after 30 kilometres picked up by bus and taken to relatively calm place. The home town of his mother has been completely evacuated.

Another letter from Scourmont (Fr Robert) dated the 18th says the remainder of the Community have left the monastery in small groups.

June 1st. Another visit from Belgian soldiers billeted in Tenby. They await orders to return to France or elsewhere.

June 3rd. New group of Belgian visitors, among them fellow countrymen and even distant relations of Community members.

June 4th. Two letters from Fr Herman. The first (9th May) tells how, after travelling all over Belgium, he finally met up with his brother Fr Desiré at Tongres. The second (21st May) from Brittany in France where he was evacuated when the Germans took Tongres. He was with the sick and so escaped their hands. He fears that Fr Desiré may have been taken prisoner—as also another monk from Scourmont. He is worried, too, about his family.

Here at Caldey it is necessary to pick up the potatoes. They are becoming black and we should take them in if we are to keep them.

June 6th. Letter from Fr Edmund read in the refectory. He is well and thinks his mother has been evacuated.

Reims has been bombarded.

Letter also from Fr Corneille, Superior of the Scourmont group who have found refuge at Notre Dame de Thymadeuc in France. ('Monk-Soldiers in Exile'). The Cistercian nuns have also had to leave, some on foot and others in lorries.

At this time it seems the monastery at Scourmont remains intact.

It seems that at 9.30 p.m. many on the Island saw a submarine in the Caldey area. Towards 11.0 p.m. a body of coastguards armed with rifles patrolled in case of attack. The Community knew nothing of this until the following morning. All this morning great aerial activity.

June 10th. In the middle of news broadcasting this morning an interruption to announce Mussolini declared war on France and her allies. Letter from Fr Benedict—he is newly equipped and ready to go to the front.

June 13th. Letters from Frs Edmund and Anselm—both experiencing enemy bombardments.

June 14th. From today in Great Britain the church bells will not ring unless the country is invaded. The silence impresses one, like days of great mourning as on Good Friday. Small hand bells used in the cloister will announce the offices of the Church.

June 15th. Paris occupied by the Germans! Here are some specimens of information received on 'Radio Journal'. It is the intention (of the Germans) to save the poor from famine and misery in attacking the custodians of wealth. They intend to be kind and indulgent to the countries conquered. All the countries so far involved are happy—Poland, Norway, Holland, Belgium. The Austrians are devoted to the German cause. Conclusion— French citizens, do not be led astray by the lying press of the English and the Jews. Come to us with faith and confidence!

June 16th. From this morning it is obvious that the meetings of French Ministers are becoming grave and serious. At 12.30 the radio announced that Marshal Petain, who was now President of the Council, had stated that France, having fulfilled its obligations towards its allies, ought now to cease fighting, and that he had asked the enemy for honourable conditions of peace. 6 p.m. news there was not much more except that negotiations should take place at Bordeaux, and that Hitler would have to see his friend Mussolini first.

June 18th, 19th and 20th. We await the outcome of events. During the talks, that Hitler does not hurry to conclude, France struggles on with courage.

June 28th. Following all the week the talks and conclusions of the armistice between France and Germany and Italy. Here in England they hope to help the French and the French colonies into revolt.

June 29th. Feast of St Peter and St Paul. Fr Odo, the Sub-Prior, celebrates his 45th anniversary in the priesthood. Unable to say High Mass alone, it was celebrated for him, but he was able to assist.

July 2nd. 8 a.m. Lecture by Fr Dominic, one of the Caldey A.R.P. wardens, on the methods of Air Raid Protection and the organisation necessary to deal with emergencies.

July 6th. Week passed packing all inessential things away for safety. It was as though the Community expected to be evacuated.

July 16th. Enemy aircraft seem to be visiting this country more often. The French and Belgian monks have to complete more and more forms in detail—their civilian jobs, their family, their relations with Germany!

July 21st, 22nd and 23rd. We hear the roar of aircraft overhead. We wait in vain (happily) for the siren to send us underground.

Aug 10th. French members of the Community have to sign papers for the Consul that they have no intention of returning to France, but if they have to they wish to be sent to the monastery at Aiguebelles.

Aug 12th. Harvest begins.

Aug 19th. While we were gathering in the barley at 3 p.m. the sirens at Tenby sounded the alert. Enemy aircraft bombing at Pembroke Dock and have set an oil tank alight. A great column of black smoke is seen and it stretches out to sea.

Aug 20th. During the night enemy aircraft pass over the Island. At 10 a.m. the wind blows the fumes from Pembroke over us, obscures the sky, and leaves an unpleasant smell.

Feast of St Bernard. We sang some of the Divine Office, but worked at the harvest this afternoon.

Aug 28th. Arrival of coal boat after many delays and problems. It remained at some distance from our depot and the discharging was very hard and very long. We worked from 4 a.m. to 9 p.m. off-loading.

Sept 4th. Almost every night the enemy visits this corner—one of the principal parts of Swansea bombed.

Oil tanks at Pembroke Dock still burning.

Sept 8th. Radio says London bombed all night. 400 dead and 1,300 to 1,400 wounded. Germans lost 85 planes to 20 English.

Sept 10th. Mr Winston Churchill announced on the radio that it appeared that the invasion of Great Britain was imminent. He exhorted all to be ready, courageous and confident, and that the following week might well be one of the most important in the history of the country.

Sept 25th. *Fire at the South Wing of the Monastery.*

At 7 p.m. while the Community were in the study room listening to the news on the radio, the cry of 'fire, fire' was heard in the cloisters. Thick smoke was pouring out of the room above the common room of the lay brothers. It was thought we could break in through the roof as the corridor was filled with smoke, and use the extinguishers, but it was beyond the elementary means at our disposal. It was necessary now to contain and save as much as possible and prevent the fire spreading. We were able to save the altar linen and the breviaries, but the flames penetrated the church and it was necessary to try to prevent the flames reaching the chapter house, parlour and entrance at one end and the refectory, Fr Prior's room and the guest-house at the other. This task took more than two hours and when the fire brigade arrived with a group of volunteer soldiers all the south wing, from the church entrance to the guest-house, was a burning mass. It was almost midnight before we could be sure that the fire was under control and not likely to spread to other sides. Then only did the monks and the Islanders, who had worked so hard with the Community, take some rest. The fire brigade continued their work and did not cease until 6 a.m. the following morning. They finally left the Island at 9 a.m.

The cause of the fire was not definitely clear—but it was not an incendiary bomb.

The damage was important since this wing contained so much of the living quarters. Of the church, the choir stalls, the high altar and the organ, nothing remained but the walls. The room of Fr Odo, his library, the stocks of papers, exercise books, register of Masses, etc. all the library with its large volumes of Holy Scripture, commentaries, theology, and classical works given by Mrs Bland, great collection of reviews—*The Month*, *Tablet*, etc, a considerable number· of devotional books, biographies, and history, the common room and refectory of the familiars, Br Teilo's room—of all these things nothing remained. One of the most critical moments was when we believed that the whole monastery might be engulfed in the flames and we began to empty the rest of the house of all that was movable.

Sept 26th. After the Masses we began to put things in order a little and to collect the things we had put out to various places the night before. The police visited the scene. The fire continued under the debris, and monks were watching during the night in case of further danger.

Sept 27th. Rising only at 5 a.m. Matins and Lauds recited privately, the Little Hours recited in common in the chapter house, private Masses celebrated in St David's Church and the chapel of the guest-house.

Sept 28th. Various places considered for a temporary church (with access available for the Islanders)—the large lounge in the guest-house, the corridor called the 'station' between the cloisters and the chapter house. This place finally chosen.

Visit of an architect and agent from the insurance company, 'The Edinburgh Assurance', who were very kindly disposed.

Sept 29th. Afternoon, after the Office of None, we walked in silence to West Beacon Point for a change of air.

Oct.—Many messages of sympathy addressed to the Community. The General Officer Commanding the Belgian army in England offered the help of a dozen men to help with the work.

At a sale in the neighbourhood of Carmarthen we purchased a black horse of 4 years old and 6 cows. Bad weather prevented us bringing them over.

Oct 15th. Arrival of Belgian soldiers. Two of them will work as joiners.

Oct 17th. Mr Mercer of Cardiff, architect for the insurance company, spent two days at Caldey with two colleagues to estimate damage.

Oct 21st. At last the cows purchased on the 12th have arrived.

Oct 23rd. Horse purchased on the 12th finally here.

Nov 14th. Arrival of a provisional high altar for the temporary church (at the 'station'), very simple, of beautiful oak. Gift of Mrs Roch. Arrival of Fr Christopher, monk of Notre Dame de Mont Cats (North France), wounded soldier and sent to England for demobilisation. Purchased seats, candlesticks, cupboards, etc, etc, from the sale at St Catherine's Fort off Tenby.

Nov.—We have received many books for the library as a result of an appeal made in the Catholic Press by Fr Daniel of Pembroke, Fr Moran of Llanelli and Fr Burton of Tenby. Miss James-Howard of Caldey, now almost blind, has given nearly all her library. The Cistercian Abbeys of Mt St Bernard, Mt Melleray and Roscrea have promised their assistance.

Nov 16th. 250 Volumes received from Mt St Bernard.

Dec 24th. By much work executed by two (and sometimes four) Belgian soldier joiners and Mr Dolby, we have a good provisional church. Wood from the wreck of the 'Bel Pareil' has been used and this smells of petrol.

Midnight Mass solemnly celebrated, many of the Islanders assisted and, as has been the custom, had their 'revillon' in the guest-house.

Dec 25th. 11.30 to midday on the radio we heard the Office of Tierce and the beginning of Pontifical High Mass from the Cistercian Monastery of Roscrea in Ireland.

At 1 p.m., as usual, we heard the news, and with satisfaction that the night and morning had passed without incident this Christmas. At 3 p.m. we listened to H.M. King George VI sending his good wishes to the people of Great Britain and the Allies.

Dec 27th. This evening Fr Prior gave some interesting news received today. Two letters received from a monk of Mont des Cats, demobilised and now at Bonnecombe. These were written on 25th November and were sent through Spain. They say that Br Andrew is also at Bonnecombe and two other monks at Scourmont.

He gave news, too, of other French monasteries—Septfons and Citeaux.

Finally he suggests communicating through the Spanish Monastery of 'Viaceli'.

1941

Jan 1st. Snow falls this first day of the year.

Jan 4th. A letter of sympathy received from Dom Aelred Carlyle in Vancouver who had news of the fire from one of the monks of the Anglican Community at Caldey, Peter Anson. He says that part of the wing destroyed was the oldest of the original buildings.

Jan 6th. Anniversary of the foundation but nothing in particular to note.

Jan 16th. The cook, Br Stanislaus, called up for medical. Convinced he would not be taken, he left without any immediate necessities. However, he was kept at Tenby without chance to return, and the boat waited in vain. That same evening the boatmen met him in Tenby in uniform and clean-shaven! He returned to Caldey every Sunday for the first month.

Feb 23. Br Stanislaus posted to Carmarthen. In a letter he says food and lodging not as good as Tenby.

March 29th. Letter from Belgian Ministry of Defence in reply to our requests for the demobilisation of Br Stanislaus, but they say they are in particular need of stretcher-bearers and infirmarians. However, they offer help for agricultural work from soldiers or men demobilised from the camp at Tenby.

March 30th. Fr Prior announced the purchase of a new boat, the 'Crimson Rambler'. It will be more comfortable for passengers, easier for carrying merchandise and beasts, and will afford more protection for the boatmen.

He announced also the settlement of the Insurance Company as a result of the fire to be satisfactory. But new difficulties now arise as money is of less value. Obviously, to purchase the materials for construction would be better now, but this is very difficult if not impossible. On the other hand, to invest the money might only produce paper.

The new Bishop of the diocese, Mgr Hannon, replied to our good wishes with a message of esteem for the contemplative life and the prayers of the Cistercians.

Apr 2nd. News from Fr Edmund at Toulouse dated 30th Dec 1940. In June he was taken prisoner but towards the end of the year he managed to escape. He spent Christmas at Notre Dame de Désert and hopes to reach Bonnecombe. Fr Benedict was taken prisoner at Compiègne and maybe is in a concentration camp. Fr Anselm was at Aiguebelle. Fr Edmund heard from Br Andrew (who had read an article in *La Croix*) that the church and library had been destroyed at Caldey. He writes that Scourmont was completely evacuated for a month and was shelled but still stands. 18 monks have returned there including Fr Herman. At Citeaux also all the monks have returned except for 15 now prisoners-of-war.

Apr 3rd. Br Stanislaus on leave for 8 days.

Apr 10th. Good Friday. Psalter recited in two hourly sessions with quarter hour breaks.

Apr 15th. About 2.40 a.m. enemy aircraft passed overhead and bombed Milton. Enemy returned later and new detonations heard about 3.30 a.m. We heard later that 15 soldiers and civilians were killed.

Apr 17th. Between 9 and 9.30 p.m. an aeroplane flying low dropped 5 or 6 flares. One fell near to St Philomena's and set the bushes on fire. At this, the intrepid officers of the Caldey A.R.P. hastened to the place armed with fire extinguishers and hand pumps.

Alas, on arrival all was extinct.

Rationing beginning to be more and more felt.

May 12th. Two side altars now finished for our temporary church, and private Masses will be said there in future instead of at St David's Church.

We are collecting a great quantity of seagulls' eggs which we will conserve.

May 19th. Two more Belgian monks called to London for mobilisation—Fr Peter went immediately and (after a journey of 10 hours) was accepted as infirmarian. Posted to a camp near Tenby. Fr Dominic also received his papers.

May 22nd. Fr Jerome in his turn went to London where he was declared fit for auxiliary service but not mobilised immediately.

June 2nd. Cheque received from the insurance company (Deo Gratias!). Letter from Fr Edmund dated 25th Feb. He acknowledges letter from Caldey (4th Dec 1940) and another one sent through Spain. Fr Anselm and Fr Thomas have been able to get back to Chimay. No news of Fr Benedict prisoner in Germany. At Bonnecombe he works in the clothing room and as cantor. Dom John, the Abbot of Bonnecombe, also enclosed a card with his letter.

June 24th. Fr Paul called to London—but he asks for a deferment.

July 3rd. Both boatmen give notice. Mr Rogers expecting to be called up decides to go now and try to get a place in the Navy. Mr Wyatt, assistant boatman, hopes to find another job. To provide for the needs of Caldey, arrangements are made with the coast-guards and the lifeboat. Our boats are anchored near the quay at Caldey. Br Thomas spent the nights there for some time.

July 5th. Fr Odo, Sub-Prior, had another stroke at 7.30 p.m. Br Thomas left for Tenby at 9 p.m. to get the doctor and also to contact the police. This was to make enquiries about an English deserter who had spent the night at the guest-house and had left, taking the contents of the alms boxes at St David's and St Illtyd's.

From then on we had only four monks at the Little Office of Our Lady at 2.0 a.m. and for meditation. One or two others joined the Canonical office.

July 10th and 11th. Coal boat discharged (114 tons). Thanks to help of three Belgian soldiers staying at Caldey we were able to off-load in two tides.

July 18th. As a result of the request for a deferment for Fr Paul, the Belgian authorities have given him until 24th Sept in order that he may work here over the harvest.

Feast of St Samson. Dinner at the guest-house for those employed by the monastery.

Aug 20th. Fr Peter on leave and sang the High Mass.

Aug 31st. Br Stanislaus also has eight days. He spent the first half at Mt St Bernard and the second at Caldey. As the harvest was beginning he asked for additional leave and one extra month was given him. He worked in the kitchen and made enough jam for the year.

The month of August was very bad and the work in the fields very much behind. Haymaking was not completed and the quality of that saved is not good.

Sept 1st. Arrival of two students from Swansea as volunteers for the harvest. Weather drier and we were able to complete in eight days. We took thirty rabbits from each of two fields.

Sept 11th. First message received directly via the Red Cross from the Abbey of Scourmont. It was signed Anselm and read—'Monastery intact, all well. Your Brothers Herman, Benedict, Anselm and Andrew here, Edmund at Bonnecombe. Six are prisoners!'

Sept 21st. Letter read in the refectory from the monastery of 'St Marie du Mont', France. It told of the bombing of the Abbey in the last days of May 1940.

Sept 25th. Anniversary of the fire. Fr Prior decided that the High Mass should be celebrated in thanksgiving for the small extent of the disaster. He told us also that the insurance is finally settled and the money would be invested in National Defence Bonds at 2½%.

Oct 6th. By reason of the small numbers of parishioners, difficulties of black-out and heating, and small number of priests, it was decided to close St David's temporarily and advance the time of the Community Mass so that all could assist.

Dec 23rd. News of the death of Dom Bonaventure de Groote, the Abbot of St Sixte and Fr Immediate of Scourmont. News received from Mt St Bernard who in return had heard this from Rome.

Fr Paul receives further deferment. This is the third or fourth time and will again continue for three months.

Dec 25th. Midnight Masses now discontinued in England due to 'black-out'. After consultation, Mass was said at this time but there was no 'reveillon' in the guest-house for the Islanders.

At 11.30 a.m. we listened to the Mass broadcast from our monastery of Roscrea in Ireland.

1942

Jan—The difficulties of transport [the boat] become greater, crossings rarer, damage often and expenses increase.

Problems must be a subject for prayers of the Community.

Jan 16th. During the night condition of Fr Odo, Sub-Prior, gave cause for anxiety. Fr Prior administered the Last Sacraments and the Community recited the prayers for the dying.

Jan 17th. 9.50 Fr Odo died without having regained consciousness. He was taken to the church about 11.0 a.m. Night watching by the body at two hour stretches taken by different monks. Night Office celebrated according to custom. Br Thomas left for Tenby with the doctor (who could only confirm death), to obtain the necessary documents for burial.

Jan 21st. The Rev Fr Francis Moncrieff, Prior of the Dominican Priory at Hawkesyard, due to preach the Retreat, unable to cross from Tenby due to bad sea.

Jan 22nd and 23rd. No boat, no preaching, no Retreat!

Jan 24th. At last at 10.30 a.m. the boat and preacher arrived.

Feb 9th. Fr Prior and the Brother Cellarer went to London on business. First consultations on financial matters and secondly questions relative to the military call-up of the Belgian and French monks. During the trip of eight days and an extra day's wait at Tenby, Fr Prior had not been at all well. Returning, he rested for several days, taking the advice of a doctor he had seen in London.

Feb 27th. The condition of Fr Prior deteriorated. He retired during the High Mass and a little later the doctor was sent for. Arriving towards evening he diagnosed a serious kidney condition and without hope of a recovery. While he was there the Prior became unconscious. Fr President (no Sub-Prior had been appointed after the death of Fr Odo) anointed him about 6.0 p.m. After Compline he told the Community of the grave condition of Fr Prior.

Feb 28th. Rev Fr Prior died about 5.20 a.m. This blow, so sudden, was a blow for everyone, as much for the Islanders as for the monks. The body was taken to the church and remained there until the next day.

Mar 1st. The Requiem Mass was sung after Prime, Vespers for the dead recited at 3.0 p.m. followed by the burial. We would have liked to have waited until the next day (Monday) and perhaps given greater solemnity to the first Titular Prior of Caldey, but with so many difficulties of travelling on a Sunday in England, and with the sea so uncertain, to say nothing of the problem with such a small Community to keep vigil, it was decided to bury at once. In fact there was no boat March 1st, 2nd or 3rd even to allow us to send the telegrams, letters and notices required.

Mar 2nd. At the Chapter, Fr Jerome (now Superior) urged the Community, after the recent deaths of both Prior and Sub-Prior, to draw together in charity and the regular life.

Mar 4th. Calmer weather enabled the boat to come to Caldey. Among the letters are those from Dom Mulachy Brazil, Abbot of Mt St Bernard, and Dom Wilfred Upson, O.S.B., Abbot of Prinknash. Both had journeyed to Tenby, but failed to cross, and had been forced to return to their monasteries without being present for the funeral of Fr Prior.

Mar 5th. Letter also from Mgr Hannon, Bishop of Menevia, offering help in case of need, and especially willing to approach the

Belgian authorities to try to prevent the 'call-up' of the remaining Belgians and, above all, the mobilisation of Fr Jerome.

Mar 8th. Fr Peter arrives on leave but is recalled almost immediately.

Mar 11th. Letter from Fr Edmund. He has received news of the death of Fr Prior and has notified Scourmont, the family Lefevre, and other Communities with whom he is in contact.

The boat lost in a thick fog and took more than two hours to reach Caldey.

Apr 5th. Good Friday passed normally in spite of our small numbers and our difficulties. Did not sing as much because of so many colds. Barefooted only between Tierce and the Mass. Dinner of bread and tea only.

Apr 21st. Received a letter dated April 24th with information that Dom Anselm Le Bail is sick and that they have evacuated the monastery and taken refuge at Notre Dame de la Paix at Chimay.

May 7th. First visit of Mgr Hannon. Speaking to the monks he offered his sympathy in the recent losses and the continual mobilisation of the Community. He encouraged all to persevere in the regular life. Sacrifices are never without some purpose.

June 1st. Boat finally arrived to collect twenty tons of cereals. 180 sacks loaded on the beach at low tide and she was able to sail for Tenby as soon as the tide rose.

June 4th. Feast of Corpus Christi. Procession took place, with altars at the village church and the post office. No visiting priests, but the nuns and some boarders came from the Tenby convent.

June 7th. Like the herd of swine in the gospel, the herd of calves at Caldey fell into the sea, more or less at the bottom of little Drinkim Bay. Out of eight, two were killed, two had broken legs and four were safe.

June 10th. From a letter received from Fr Edmund it appears that the monks of Scourmont have again had to evacuate from the chateau of the Prince of Chimay where they had taken refuge. Now they are with the Christian Brothers of Momignies. They were able to rescue the contents of the sacristy and the library, also some provisions, but were forced to leave the farming materials, livestock and brewery equipment.

June 9th. More problems with the boat. The quay at Tenby will be closed. It is necessary to seek permission for the boats to have right of entry and to arrange anchorage. Also to keep our right to use the store. In addition we need some arrangement for a crane and we hope that the military might repair the broken one at Caldey. This project did not result in anything.

July 11th. Return of Fr Paul with leave for six months. It is hoped

Br Stanislaus will have the same favour. Success to some steps taken by so many friends of Caldey.

July 13th. Br Stanislaus returned for six months.

July 27th. Fr Peter on leave for eight days.

Aug 18th. Twelve invasion barges arrive at Tenby, but leave for Pembroke the next day.

Aug 19th. The absence of a crane at Tenby means a return to the old method of transporting cattle from Tenby to Caldey, i.e. to make the beasts swim behind the boats.

Sept 3rd. Arrival of Dom Celsus O'Connell, Abbot of Mount Melleray in Ireland. Dom Celsus gave the Community news of some of our monasteries and recommended all to the prayers of the Community. The monks in Japan had dispersed. Westmalle, like Scourmont, had been evacuated. Some monks from Mt St Bernard had to leave and serve as parish priests and chaplains.

Sept 25th. Three M.P's. visit Caldey and Br Thomas explained our difficulties in keeping contact with the mainland without a telephone and also the need for a crane at Tenby.

Oct 4th. Telegram received from Fr Edmund. In this Dom Anselm of Scourmont confirms that Fr Jerome has all the powers of Superior.

Oct 13th. Letter from Dom Anselm announcing for the fourth time that Fr Jerome is Superior at Caldey as he himself is at Scourmont. He asked that we keep a family life as they are trying to do in their situation as evacuees. All are well—Fr Anselm Payen is not yet ordained.

Oct 16th. Visit from Dom Malachy Brazil, Abbot of Mt St Bernard, when he spoke with most of the individual monks and visited the monastery and farm. He addressed the assembled Community and spoke with much admiration for what was being accomplished, the observance of the Rule, etc., etc., especially with so small a number of monks.

Oct 27th. Further information from Dom Anselm Le Bail through Fr Edmond on the authority now vested in Fr Jerome. He says he has permission—as also Br Andrew—to return to Caldey but doubts the possibility. He has already taken certain steps but without success.

Oct 30th. We feared the requisition of the boat by the Royal Navy, but afterwards we understood they had taken some others and did not want the 'Crimson Rambler'. It is becoming more and more difficult to keep the boat at Tenby due to the regulations at the quay and the boatmen offer to keep it at a mooring at Caldey. Permission given to use an R.A.F. buoy until we had a buoy nearer to the quay at Caldey. When the bad weather makes this impossible we will anchor at Tenby.

Nov 1st. Fr Jerome spoke this morning, officially as it were, as Superior of the Community. He recalled that it was eight months since the decease of Dom Aelred and since that time he had in fact directed the Community. However, since the information received from Father Immediate (Dom Anselm) had been more explicit and, after consultations with the Abbots of Mt Melleray and Mt St Bernard, he accepted the situation as official Superior with the normal rights and responsibilities. In consequence he appointed Fr Francis Giraudot as second Superior with the title of Sub-Prior. He thanked the Community for their help and devotion which had so far enabled them to live the life regularly and celebrate the Divine Offices in choir. He asked all to continue, not only to seek personal perfection, but to maintain always their efforts to make the common life one of love and self-sacrifice.

Nov 3rd. Long letter from Fr Edmund read out in the refectory. It is astonishing that the French censors allow all this literature to pass in Great Britain.

Nov 10th. Invasion of French Africa by the Americans.

Nov 13th. Rest of France taken over by the Germans.

Nov 15th. In order to celebrate the recent victories of the Allies in Egypt and Lybia we have sung a Te Deum and the Islanders some verses of 'God Save the King'. The bells, too, have been rung as the ban was lifted on this occasion. As Mr Churchill said, 'It was the END of the beginning of the war'.

Nov 30th. Message from Dom Anselm through the Red Cross says, for the fifth time, 'Repeat that Fr Jerome is Superior and he authorises the Abbot of Mt St Bernard to make the Visitation'. (It is clear this time).

Dec 13th. A very heavy sea has been the cause of considerable damage. The large barge and two small boats at the quay of Caldey have been destroyed. Luckily the 'Crimson Rambler' anchored at Eel Point has been spared. At Tenby also considerable damage has been done and nearly all the small craft have been destroyed.

Dec 25th. Night office was recited only and Mass celebrated without deacon or sub-deacon. No 'reveillon' for the Islanders after Mass. Admiral Darlan has been assassinated in Africa and .... at Caldey a cow has strangled itself.

1943
Jan 8th. Terrible storms. No boat for five days in spite of need of doctor for an Islander.

Jan 11th. Death of Dom Herman Joseph Smets—Abbot General of our Order. News received through an article in the *Catholic Times*.

Jan 29th. The Abbot of Mt St Bernard telephoned the coastguards (in Tenby) to check the state of the sea before starting off on his regular Visitation. He was put off by the bad weather and delayed his visit for a fortnight.

Feb 22nd. Arrival of the Abbot of Mt St Bernard and his Sub-Prior, Fr Hugh Talbot.

Feb 24th. Opening of the Regular Visitation. The last was 1939. The Abbot Visitor recalled the delegation of authority from the Rev Abbot of Scourmont. He commented on the text from the Day's gospel, 'Come to me all you who labour and I will refresh you'. He addressed the lay brothers during the evening.

Feb 26th. The Abbot Visitor stated that not only was there satisfaction for him, but admiration for what was being done in spite of their small number.

Mar 25th. Letter from Fr Edmund received via Roscrea. Br Andrew very happy at Citeaux—Fr Edmund hopes to rejoin the Scourmont Community—Fr Benedict has fallen and injured his head.

Apr 21st. Good Friday spent very quietly—the Books of Psalms not recited.

May 3rd. This evening the boat 'Crimson Rambler' has been torn from its mooring by the storm and thrown on the rocks at Eel Point.

May 4th. All attempts to refloat it the next day were in vain.

May 9th. We learn that the other boat 'Stephen Harding' had made the shelter of the harbour at Tenby.

What a week of anxiety! . . .

May 21st. 36 rabbits caught in the place of the old poultry house. We have declared a war this spring against the rodents. Another innovation—electric fencing to divide the fields. The beasts become sensitive to this at once.

June 24th. 'Corpus Christi'—No open air procession.

June 25th. Small cargo (65 tons) of coal discharged between 3.45 and 9.45 p.m. fairly easy even with so few workers.

June 26th. Letter from Fr Ides of Scourmont—Community back at the Monastery.

July 2nd. All non-residents to leave the area, now to be counted as a closed zone, from July 6th next.

July 21st. Many invasion barges arrive at Tenby. Germans broadcast on the radio that they are aware of the invasion build-up in the Bristol Channel.

July 26th. Finished the haymaking thanks to good weather. However, with so much work, we asked for help with weeding from the ladies (the 'land girls' of Caldey) and Miss Alice Smith, Mrs Shand and Miss Grossé showed their devotion to Caldey.

Aug 14th. A fact worthy of note in the records of Caldey Abbey. For the first time (maybe not the last!) merchandise loaded at Tenby has been off-loaded, not at the quay, but in the centre of the Island at the foot of the monastery. This was done by an amphibious tank or invasion barge.

Aug 31st. Finished cutting the harvest. Weather has been wet all the month and has made the work long and difficult. However, half the wheat and a third of the barley is inside.

Sept 2nd. Message received from Fr Albert Derzelle, Prior of Chimay. He says there are seven novices and many postulants.

Oct 16th. The boatman, Mr Cook, finished work with us. Br Thomas, helped by Fernand Lenterne, did what he could to look after the boat (anchored near Caldey quay).

Nov 6th. The boat, returning to Tenby, has not been able to be tied up at the normal buoy. It has been taken up by the waves and thrown onto the beach. They had to dig round it and wait for the high tide before refloating. They finally succeeded without damamge.

Dec 1st. A long letter from Fr Edmund (sent Nov 3rd) read out at Compline. It tells of the death of Fr Lazare. News of Fr Herman of Caldey. Community of Scourmont out again at Momignies where is much work and the harvest was good. Nobody departed for work in Germany. He gives a list of books he has bought for Caldey.

Dec 25th. Christmas. Night office was recited only. Midnight Mass celebrated by the Superior. Many people assisted and the *communicants* were many. The Community only took the 'reveillon' but were unable to do anything for the Islanders. However, a distribution of meat was especially appreciated.

1944

Jan 10th. Fr Paul and Br Stanislaus receive a deferment from a re-call.

Jan 31st. Message by Red Cross from Fr Herman dated Oct 25th, 1943—'News Caldey well received always. Health good. Stayed with Community. Edmund, Anselm at Bonnecombe, Andrew at Citeaux. Kind regards to all. Respects to Fr Prior.'

Mar 2nd. Visit of M.P. Delighted with his 'cruise' he left a modest cheque and promised to send some biscuits made in his factory.

Mar 4th. Message by Red Cross sent by family of one of the Community—'Eight monks of Momignies have been sent to the prison of Brussels!'

Mar 6th. Fr Jerome, the Superior, received his call-up papers for the Belgian Army (March 27th). In the meanwhile he has contacted the Bishop, Apostolic Delegate, the Abbots, Committee for Agriculture, etc. . .

Mar 7th. Letter from M. Jacobs says that the Belgian authorities are making a review of all those not yet called up. He assures us that he will do everything possible for the Community and will speak to M. Peirlot himself.

Mar 18th. Message received from Dom Anselm, Abbot of Scourmont, from Momignies (Jan 5th)—'We continue the religious life here. I remain contented about you. Blessings. . . Le Bail'.

Also message received from Fr Herman—'Fr Benedict myself with you in Spirit on this Anniversary of the Caldey foundation'. Finally telegram from Labour office at Haverfordwest says Fr Jerome's call-up now off and letter from Belgian Ambassador to follow.

Mar 21st. Fr Peter, chaplain to the Navy, back here for a month's leave. First leave in 13 months.

Mar 22nd. Message received from Fr Colomban (Jan 5th) instructing us to prayer No: 33 in the missal. Dom Anselm well.

Apr 1st. Message from Fr Robert (Dec 31st, 1943) says that the situation at Scourmont is very serious. Fr Thomas and Fr Albert very sick and isolated. Fr Robert thought to have some sickness. Eleven monks missing. Fr Abbot depressed.

Apr 2nd. Reading in the refectory of two letters dated Christmas 1943. First from Fr Edmund with news of Scourmont, the second from Fr Anselm who writes of his theological studies with a monk from Tilbourg as his teacher. He finishes with some spiritual notes on peace in the heart.

Apr 22nd. Message from the Red Cross on behalf of the Abbey of Chimay tells us that the missing have turned up safe and well and hope to be back for Easter.

Apr 24th. Extracts from a letter from Fr Ides written to his aunts, the Misses Grossé. In it he explains the arrest of some monks at Scourmont. This was due to the denouncement of them by a pro-German Choir oblate (a 'Germanophile' who finished his letters with 'Heil Hitler'). He left Scourmont remembering well the names of those he especially disliked. It seems he then made a report to the Gestapo. This was followed by a visit from armed soldiers to Momignies (where the Community had taken refuge) and all identity cards were examined. One tenth of the religious were taken away and the others released.

He gave other news of the Community and details of the office and work.

May 14th, 15th and 16th. Fearing the impossibility of transportation we have been much occupied with the despatch of all the grain we have to sell.

May 17th. Arrival of Dom Malachy from Mt St Bernard for the regular Visitation.

May 21st. Termination of the visit and the Abbot exhorted all to seek an interior life and union with God.

June 25th. Rome has been taken by the Allies. Thank God. Invasion of France between Cherbourg and Le Havre—more than 4,000 ships without counting barges, and 10,000 aircraft. Unbelievable.

This evening the Allies reached Caen without great opposition.

June 28th. Corpus Christi. Procession in the village with very few visitors but very successful in its calm and piety.

The children of the Island sang well.

July 1st. Message from Fr Colomban that the last two captives, Fr Albert and Fr Thomas, both back with the Community, also Jubilee [of] Fr Samuel—great celebrations.

Aug 3rd. Harvest begins. Magnificent weather.

Aug 14th. Letter from Fr Peter tells us he is in Normandy. He says he was deeply moved to put his feet on French soil again after seven years. He has been well received and especially when they know he is 'Un petit Belge'.

Sept 9th. Finished the harvest of barley near Sandtop Bay.

We follow with interest the progress of the Allies since the invasion. Things are moving fast in France and Belgium, and we may hope soon to have news of our Monasteries and our families.

Sept 15th. Arrival of Br Martin, an English brother from Notre Dame de Thymadeuc. He has left France to avoid being taken prisoner by the Germans.

Sept 17th. Princess Tira, niece of King Zog of Albania, visited Caldey. She assisted at the High Mass although she is a Mohammedan. Four members of her family are Catholic and she is thinking of becoming one. After coffee in the guest-house she visited the Old Priory and walked as far as Sandtop Bay with an English officer. She left about mid-day enchanted with her visit.

Sept 23rd. Opening of Community Retreat preached by Fr Devas, S.J.

Sept 26th. Letter from Fr Peter says he was able to visit Scourmont for about one hour and a half. He saw Dom Anselm who had suffered a lot. Monastery not badly damaged. During the occupation the refectory had been a cinema and the chapter house served as a bar. The church remained closed, but the organ had been dismantled by Belgian workers who had taken all the electrical parts. He had not seen any of the 'Caldeyans'. He thought the Abbot would send a new contingent to Caldey. The guest-house full of Americans.

Sept 27th. Letter received from Dom Anselm dated Sept 14th. The Germans left 'in a hurry' at mid-day, Sept 2nd. The monks returned in the evening and found the monastery in good condition. They began immediately the regular life and sang the day offices in the church, but those of the night in the chapter house on account of the black-out. Harvest had been made by the Community without help, 50 acres had been cultivated and there remain six acres of potatoes to gather in. Figures at Jan 1st were 64 monks of whom 52 were priests, 22 lay brothers. Total of 86. Four died 1943.

All goes well at Notre Dame de la Paix. Trappistines at Chimay. Frs Charles, Samuel and Sebastian are there as chaplains.

The 'Caldeyans' at Scourmont are well. They will begin theological studies again soon with Frs Thomas, Emanuel and Maur as Teachers.

Sept 29th. Our Retreat closed. The subject had been the great love of God for man and how necessary it is to return this love by avoidance of sin, practising the virtues and having confidence in Him. He (Fr Devas) spoke very quickly in English and this necessitated some effort for us to follow him. His sermons were deeply spiritual, especially his explanation of many scenes taken from the gospels.

Dec—More news from members of the Caldey Community. Fr Benedict writes from the convent at Chimay. Fr Anselm and Fr Edmund return to Scourmont.

Br Andrew, too, writes from Citeaux—Dom Godefroid, the Abbot, also adds a few words.

Dec 4th. Fr Paul, worried about the renewal of leave for himself and Br Stanislaus, has gone to London.

Dec 13th. Message from Red Cross reports deaths of Fr Maxime and Fr Samuel at Scourmont.

Dec 25th. Christmas—nothing different from preceding years.

Dec 29th. Letter from Fr Herman in the care of a young man from the Chimay area who has arrived at Caldey. This letter contains details of the German occupation of the Monastery. The cellars of the brewery contained explosives which the enemy wanted to blow up but after a parley it was agreed to transfer them into the fields. They left blankets, boots, etc., etc., but sent a lorry later to collect most of them.

The young man who brought the letter is the son of Dr André, the monastery doctor. Attached to the British Army, he had dropped by parachute and become a leader in the 'Maquis'.

There is only one more entry in the Journal after this. It is for January 1945 with a list of the Community on Caldey at the time.

9
SOME BRIEF EXPLANATIONS

*'For whatsoever things were written aforetime
were written for our learning'*: Romans 15:4

The extracts from the Journal quoted in the previous chapter
tell vividly in themselves something of the problems and
tribulations which the Community on Caldey had to endure
during the war years. As a family they were affected as other
families were, and the evidence is all there of the anxiety and
the waiting for messages, both from their own absent Brothers
and concerning the welfare of other Communities on the
Continent. Even so, a few comments and a word or two of
explanation here and there may not be out of place.

As happened in so many cases, some Brothers were more
fortunate than others in their postings and the conditions in
which they found themselves. Fr Pascal, for example, after
various vicissitudes, found himself living in some comfort and
in the midst of plenty. Yet, discharged at this time and tempted
with the opportunity of staying on to take advantage of the
easy life, he opted to return immediately to his Community, to
the hard life and the self-denial.

On the Island, those who remained were faced with many
great difficulties, not the least of which was the serious
shortage of labour. As always in the history of this country,
prosperity returned to the land in time of war as the nation
turned again to the farmers whom it had betrayed in time of
peace. Without the labour to produce, however, this temporary
prosperity was not something which the monks could easily
turn to their financial advantage. And as a result of the general
war-time exigencies, restrictions and shortages, the problems
of living and farming on an island became even more acute.
The starkness of the situation is evident in the references to the
waiting for the doctor or the veterinary surgeon, the blight
upon the potatoes and the simple statement of the fact of
working from four o'clock in the morning until nine o'clock in
the evening to unload the coal-boat.

Then, of course, as always on an island, transcending all other considerations, there was the situation with the boat. By 1942 this had assumed such desperate proportions that it had become a matter for the prayers of the Community. And, on the question of prayer, be it noted that the monks, in spite of the temporal demands upon them, continued to give a high degree of priority to their true vocation, which is, of course, one of prayer. Over and above the extra demands created by various alarums and excursions, it is evident that they were keeping at least to their normal busy daily routine of seven hours' prayer and seven hours' manual work. Except that after the awful experience of the fire, they indulged themselves, with great human frailty, in the luxury of a 'lie-on' one morning until five o'clock!

The fire was the worst single calamity to have befallen the Community since their coming to Caldey twelve years previously. There are at least two interesting points concerning this disaster, the details of which are known to very few people. One is the cause of the fire, whilst the other is the identity of the person whose actions that night were probably responsible for saving the monastery from total destruction.

In writing up the details of the fire in the Journal, Fr Bertin said that the cause of the fire was not clear, but that it was *not* an incendiary bomb. He almost certainly made this point because it is one which the police would have raised the following day since, on the night of the fire, an air raid on Swansea across the bay had been in progress. The police were no wiser than Fr Bertin as to the exact cause of the fire. It is perhaps incomprehensible to those who do not know something of the monks, but nobody would ever have known the cause unless they had happened to ask those who knew. And those who knew would not have spoken to anyone on the subject unless they were specifically asked. There is simply no small talk amongst them. At this time they would have been going about their daily tasks of praying and working, speaking only when spoken to, or when they themselves had a question to ask.

It could perhaps give some idea of this facet of a monk's make-up to quote a little incident which occurred during the course of research for this book. I was staying on the Island at the time when, after some persistent questioning on my part, Fr Dominic, one of the older monks who had come across with the original contingent from Chimay, happened to mention, quite casually, that at one time one of the monks had written in a big book about everything that happened. Enquiries with other members of the Community drew blank. They had never even heard of its existence. Nothing daunted, the next time I was in his office, I asked the Abbot if he knew anything about it. As casually as Fr Dominic, who had told me about it in the first place, he said that that must be the book way up on the top shelf of his cupboard. Underneath a thirty-years' layer of dust was the answer, beyond the wildest dreams, to any researcher's prayer. It was, of course, the book from which so many extracts have already been quoted.

During the course of that visit I showed my precious discovery to three other members of the Community, each of whom shared my excitement and enthusiasm. On my next visit, however, other members of the Community to whom I spoke still knew nothing at all about the finding of this treasure. The only ones in the monastery who are aware of it now (1974) are almost certainly those I have told, for those Brothers to whom I showed it will not have told them. There are members of the Community, in fact, who will know nothing of this record unless and until they read these pages.

There are no doubt people who will say that the monks deliberately tried to conceal the real cause of the fire. Had they wished to do this they could have allowed everybody to believe what they all seemed ready and willing to believe, that it had been caused by a stray incendiary bomb from the Swansea raid. Instead, this possibility was categorically refuted and, because nobody happened to ask one of the monks who knew, it became generally accepted that it must have been due to an electrical fault. And, of course, the Community were maintaining a greater degree of silence in those days than they do now.

At this point it would perhaps be as well to mention that, for one reason or another, monks sometimes change the name by which they are known, and assume a name which is common in their Order. Those who know some of the present Community should remember, therefore, that the present-day Fr Anselm or Fr Edmund, for example, would not necessarily be the monks of those names who were referred to in the Journal. The Fr Anselm in the Journal was, in fact, Fr Anselm Payen, who subsequently settled in Chimay. He had been the Community's bee-keeper and, when he went away to the war, he left this part of his duties to a somewhat eccentric Irishman, Fr Patrick Rafferty.

Fr Patrick was neither by inclination nor calling what might be termed a born apiarist. But he was prepared to do his best. If his best resulted in nearly burning down the entire monastery, there is no reason to believe that the gates of Heaven will be barred against him because of it. The failures in life, as it has been remarked, are those who never tried.

The time of year, it will have been noted, was late September, by which season most of the honey would already have been extracted. Fr Patrick, however, had deemed it necessary to do some fumigating of the frames on which the honeycombs are built. This he undertook with considerable enthusiasm and the aid of the tried and trusted old-fashioned sulphur candles. Carefully closing the door and the windows in the room of his operations near the church, he left the candles to do their work. One of them, at least, was too close to the wax, which caught fire. To make matters worse, there was pitch on the roof. With this, and a large supply of wax, burning furiously, it was only through a miracle and the wind being strongly in the right direction, that the whole place was not gutted before the fire-brigade from Tenby was able to arrive and prevent the fire from spreading further.

This reference to the fire-brigade on an island may be thought odd, and this is the second point about which little is generally known, and which is worth some elaboration. For reasons which have already been considered, it is probable that the monks never knew the real story of how the fire-brigade came to be on Caldey that night.

There had been no telephone on Caldey, it will be remembered, since the breaking of the cable in 1938. As the flames lit the night sky across the water it was not long before hundreds of Tenby people were watching from the Esplanade above the town's South Beach. Here, perhaps, is one of the first manifestations of the moving of the Spirit because, whereas ten years previously the attitude had been so very different, there was now everywhere deep concern for the monks and what was happening. But no-one, it seemed, could do anything. In civic matters, Caldey, for some odd and ancient reason, did not come under Tenby. It came under Pembroke. Therefore the order could not be given for the Tenby brigade to do anything. Whilst the problem was being duly considered and discussed, the fire on the Island continued to rage, whilst the monks, as the Journal records, with only 'the elementary means at their disposal', tried to put it out.

Fortunately for the monks there was one person in Tenby that night who was a doer rather than a talker. She was the late Miss Marjorie Knowling, a well-loved member of a respected Tenby family, who gave tremendous voluntary service to the community in which she lived. When, in later years, she was appointed an M.B.E., the news was received with great joy in the town as a welcome change from the reading of the monotonous lists of civil servants and political sycophants whose awards have so often made a nonsense over the years of any merit the idea may once have had.

This sort of thought was much in people's minds at that time, as a result of the huge fires at Pembroke Dock's oil storage tanks some weeks previously, and referred to in the Journal. These references will be more fully appreciated if it is realised that in this huge fire, reckoned at the time to have been the biggest since the Great Fire of London, thirty-three million gallons of oil were lost. The fire burned for nearly three weeks and was fought by twenty-two fire-brigades from all over the country. Five men from the Cardiff brigade lost their lives. When the gallantry awards were announced, one man who had spent a day on the scene in a supervisory capacity (but who subsequently declined to venture on the Caldey effort) was honoured, whilst heroes, who had fought the fire without going to bed for seventeen days and nights, had received no more than the metaphorical (and actual) bowl of hot soup and thank-you-for-coming. And the bowl of soup had been supplied by the ceaseless efforts of the women in the area. Just as in the Caldey fire five weeks later, the handful of women and girls amongst the Islanders struggled heroically to save what they could, and brewed tea even in the 'forbidden' areas where women were not normally admitted.

That night Marjorie Knowling moved heaven and earth to make it possible for the Tenby Volunteers to get the A.F.S. pump across to Caldey to fight the fire. And somehow she managed to obtain an order for the R.A.F. launch, stationed in Tenby, to be used for transport.

There was, however, no water in the harbour, but the R.A.F. launch being anchored off-shore, was afloat, and the Tenby men man-handled the pump down across the old Victoria Pier, which has since been demolished. That in itself was no mean effort in the black-out, nor was the crossing to the Island. A horse and cart were used to rush the pump from the landing jetty, whilst the lily pond in the middle of the village supplied the water. The pump was white hot by the time the fire had been brought under control, and the water level of the pond had been lowered by a couple of feet.

With further reference to the air raids and enemy aircraft activity at that time it is surprising, especially with such a lack of communication amongst themselves, that any of the monks should have known details of the air raid of April 15th in the following year. There is always a possibility that such a report could have been no more than rumour. Due to war-time reporting censorship, figures are very difficult, if not impossible, to come by. But reference to W. L. Richards' very useful and interesting booklet *Pembrokeshire Under Fire*, the only account of the air raids on Pembrokeshire during 1940 and 1941, shows that this entry is surprisingly correct in detail, except that the service men involved were possibly airmen and not soldiers.

The entry for the happenings on Caldey two nights later shows that the monks had lost neither their sense of humour nor the ability to laugh at themselves. With Br Thomas being involved, how could they?

It is with mention of Br Thomas that the reference to rationing 'beginning to be more and more felt' assumes particular significance, because it was on this subject that one of the many stories of his ready wit is to be found. By this time he had already become so much of an institution in Tenby that the formal Thomas had long since been dropped and, to the many who knew him he was, as often as not, known simply as Brother. The humorous stories about him are legion and would, on their own, fill a good chapter or even a small book.

Some of his puns were quite outrageous. But, equally, some of his wit was pure gold and so instantaneous that it must surely make the best of script-writers envious indeed.

At this time of rationing and scarcity, provisioning the Island Community was a matter of considerable difficulty. Where anything was rationed it was not too bad, because at least each man had a ration. But where things were merely scarce it was sometimes very awkward, because usually it meant being there in the queue when whatever it was that was wanted was being handed out. At this particular time toilet rolls were very difficult to obtain. The manager of Boots the chemists' Tenby branch agreed with Br Thomas that he had a particular problem in trying to cater for the needs of the Community on the Island. He acknowledged, too, that Brother could not be expected to be there waiting for the toilet rolls to come in. And so, with great magnaminity, and with the goodwill which was by now much more prevalent towards the monks, he agreed to put Brother's name down for a whole gross carton of toilet rolls.

On each of his occasional visits to the mainland, Brother would call in at Boots, and each time Mr Goldstraw, the manager, would say no, there was no news, but would urge him to be patient and to rest assured that the order was there specially for the monks and when the carton arrived it would be theirs and theirs alone.

At last the fateful day arrived when Brother walked in and Mr Goldstraw, face beaming and rubbing his hands, said, 'Good news, Brother. Good news at last.'

'Have they come?' said Brother, 'Have you got them?'

'No, not yet. We haven't got them, but the invoice came yesterday.'

'Well, for Heaven's sake,' said Brother, 'let me have that. They're getting desperate over there!'

It should not be thought from any of this that humour was the prerogative solely of Br Thomas. Once, when I was over on Caldey, I remember asking Fr Anselm whether he had ever read a certain book. 'No,' he said, 'I didn't finish it, Roscoe. I was reading it, but when I was about half way through, somebody swiped it.' Momentarily taken aback, I said, 'Well! Good gracious! You don't mean to tell me that monks actually swipe things, do they?' He thought for a few moments, then gave a wry smile that was at once both worldly and heavenly, and said, 'No. Not exactly. It's what we call Total Community.' Then he went on to tell me of the time when they started making chocolate, and Br John, the Brother responsible, gave them all a bar of chocolate each to sample. Fr Anselm decided to keep his for a rainy day and put it on the top shelf of the cupboard. Then, one day, when he no doubt thought the penance had gone far enough, he turned, squirrel-like, to his precious store. But, like the book, that, too, had been total-communitied!

It is very much a case of total community, too, as far as the gulls are concerned, as will be seen from the reference to the collecting of gulls' eggs for preserving. The two most numerous species of gulls on Caldey are the herring gulls and the lesser black-backed gulls, both of which nest on Caldey and St Margaret's, and which have been there in large numbers for many years. Their presence in such numbers is largely attributable to the ready supply of food, since they are by nature scavengers. Until comparatively recent times Tenby had a flourishing little fishing fleet, so that there was plenty of offal for the gulls. By the time the fishing industry had begun to decline, the tourist trade was increasing, and the gulls were able to turn to the even greater quantities of crude sewage being very conveniently discharged into the sea between the town's South Beach and Caldey. The town's refuse tip, too, has always played its part, whilst in the autumn and spring the birds can be seen following the ploughs in great white clouds, in search of worms on the coastal farms, and often much further inland. So that, certainly ever since the Cistercians came to Caldey, there has been this plentiful source of excellent food, free, and there for the taking.

The gulls nest on the cliffs, and on the flat cliff-tops above. Here, the nests are easily accessible. They lay their large pear-shaped eggs, brown or olive-coloured with darker speckling, in clutches of three. When the eggs are taken, the birds will lay again and will lay three times in the course of the season, so that, provided care is taken to collect the eggs when they are fresh, a good stock can be preserved. They are excellent for baking, or they can be eaten hard-boiled with salad, and many families in coastal areas prize them highly.

The invasion exercises which were carried out in the area, in preparation for the D-Day landings in Normandy, have now become a part of history, and knowledge of them is general, but when they took place in 1943 tight security measures were enforced. For the monks on Caldey the situation created all sorts of further problems and difficulties. For some time prior to this the tightening of security around harbour areas had increased their difficulties. In cold words on paper it may not convey much that it had become necessary to moor the boat at Caldey instead of at Tenby harbour. But the hazards, in fact, were automatically increased a hundredfold. The east wind is the menace for Caldey, blowing across Carmarthen Bay as it does, right into the Island's quay. It was not long before the monks lost their boat, the 'Crimson Rambler'. Nor should it be too difficult to imagine something of the rigours suffered by Br Thomas, having to spend night after night in the boats to keep watch.

Likewise, the brief mention in an earlier chapter of the bells having been taken down and sent at last to Prinknash does not in itself excite any great feeling of hardship or difficulty. To see pictures of them being loaded into the boat is to realise that life on an island can never be anything other than much more difficult than on the mainland.

By far the worst experience for the Community during these difficult years, however, must have been the loss of their beloved Prior and the Sub-Prior within six weeks of each other. When Fr Odo died, a Sub-Prior had not been appointed in his place before the Prior, Fr Aelred Lefevre, also died suddenly. Sadly depleted in numbers as they were, and with war-time communications with Chimay and the other monks being sporadic and well-nigh impossible, it must have been a severe test of the faith and moral fibre of those who remained. How they came through these ordeals is more appropriately dealt with later.

10
A TIME OF GREAT DIFFICULTY

*'Seek ye first the Kingdom of God, and His righteousness:
and all these things shall be added unto you'*: Matthew 6:33

Why Fr Bertin discontinued the writing of his most valuable
Journal when he did, at the beginning of 1945, will perhaps
now never be known. One of the problems in questioning
monks is that a good monk has no idea of dates or years. He is
so engrossed in his own life of prayer and search for God that
time matters nothing to him. Occasionally there is a big event
such as the fire, or the coronation of a monarch, or the election
of a new Abbot, and a monk will relate a much less important
happening to a time either before or after the bigger event.
Often, that is as far as he can go.

The inscription on the cross in the Island's little churchyard
says that Fr Bertinus Dumortier did not die until May 1947.
And at that time, to use the words of Fr Pascal, one of the older
French monks, 'He was not sick to die. He just died.' He was,
in fact, found in his office, where he had died of a heart attack,
in his chair. The first part of the Journal had been written,
possibly at Chimay, with much of it being taken from letters
and notes of the first Prior, Fr Andrew Garcette. Then, for a
time, Fr Rémy took over before the task was allotted to Fr
Bertin.

*[Author's note—I mentioned earlier, which was when writing this
book twenty years ago, that the Journal had evidently been written
up sporadically. Subsequently, in the course of research in the
monastery archives for my later book, Caldey, I did indeed find the
'penny exercise book' in which Fr Bertin had made his notes almost
up to the time he died, two years after he had written up his last
entries in the Journal itself—R.H.].*

On one point, however, there is no uncertainty. By the post-
war years the monks of Caldey stood at a cross-roads. Yet the
only way which it seemed feasible for them to take was to
return along the road they had come. The war years had seen
their numbers reduced to a dozen and their position now
seemed hopeless, both spiritually and temporally.

Their main objective had been to establish an English-speaking Community on Caldey. Like the man in Thomas Hood's *Past and Present* they might have thought:

> It was a childish ignorance,
> But now 'tis little joy
> To know I'm farther off from Heaven
> Than when I was a boy.

They may not have been farther off from Heaven but, monastically, the position was worse than disheartening, and the project was already being regarded as a failure. In the General Chapter of 1948, however, Dom Anselm Le Bail, Abbot of Chimay, made a strong intervention in favour of the continuation of the Community. He suffered a stroke immediately afterwards and, although he lived on for another six years, he did not speak or communicate again.

Financially, the position was just as bleak. The Community had by that time been there twenty years and, in this respect, an interesting comparison can be drawn. For the other Pembrokeshire islands, much the same in size and farming pattern as Caldey, some interesting information is available.

In the last two hundred years there is only one instance on record of anyone farming any of the other Pembrokeshire islands for more than about ten years. No attempt had been made to farm Skokholm after 1912. On Skomer and Ramsey, in the years immediately following the Second World War, there were capable farmers still trying to wrest a living from the land, but Skomer's farming was abandoned in 1950, and Ramsey's a decade or so later. There were, too, many instances of people going to the islands to farm and lasting no more than a year or two. The grass, of course, is always greener on the other side of the hedge. To farm an island appeals to many, but to succeed is given to few. It looks inviting from the mainland, but many of those who have the courage and faith to embark on such projects are not prepared for the dangers, frustrations and sometimes insurmountable hazards created by boats, rough seas and long periods of isolation, and they soon return to the mainland.

The monks, then, in the late forties, were facing serious problems on two separate fronts. Yet, in both instances, it was a case once again of 'Cometh the hour, cometh the man.' It might even have been a case of, as the old hymn has it, 'He moves in a mysterious way His wonders to perform.'

Stark tragedy though it had been for the Community to lose both Prior and Sub-Prior within six weeks of each other, at a time when their spirits must have been at a very low ebb, had it not happened it is unlikely that Dom Albert Derzelle would have been sent to Caldey to take over as Prior. Appointed in the first place, in 1946, he was subsequently elected by the Community, as Fr Aelred Lefevre had been before him. And Dom Albert Derzelle was one of the truly great men.

It has been said of him that, like the great Pope John XXIII, he was a man before his time and opened the windows to let in some fresh air. Even so, there are always the critics, and some Catholics would say that opening the window only lets in a draught. But this can more properly be discussed in a later chapter. Unquestionably, Dom Albert, a teacher largely by example, had a certain charisma and attracted to the Community a number of very able, English-speaking novices.

Not all of these novices stayed. It may come as a surprise to many people but, since society became familiar with what is known as statistical information, it has been established that out of every twenty men who become novices only one stays on to become a monk. In the immediate post-war years this very low ratio was accentuated. Many men came back from the war sickened and disillusioned, believing that monastic life might be the answer. Not surprisingly, they failed to stay the course. On the other hand, a few of them found that monasticism was their true vocation. It serves to highlight the fact that those who stay on to become monks are not just running away from life or opting out. Some may pursue such a course in the initial stages but, when they do measure up to the rigours of the life, it is because they are meant for it. Only then do they find the deep inward happiness which their calling can bring to them. It is not unusual for men to follow other vocations in life and then to change to something else, and it is no different for a monk. When he changes his mind it does not necessarily make him any worse as a man or lacking as a Christian.

Allowance having been made for this factor at this particular period, it is still evident that the intake of novices at that time was a great boost to the spiritual need of the Community, and a cause for thanks and rejoicing.

Dom Albert had himself, when in Belgium, been called up during the war when he was Prior of Chimay. The first four novices to be enrolled at Caldey after the war had been sent to Chimay for their novitiate but, when more novices arrived on the Island, these four were brought back and the future looked altogether more promising. In a matter of a few years the Community had achieved its English-speaking objective, and this in itself must have been a great help to the original members in overcoming the language problems which had always been considerable.

There remained, however, the question of financial viability. The man who came at that hour, and who probably had more to do than any other individual with turning Caldey into a successful business enterprise, was Fr Anthony ffrench-Mullen. He came to Caldey, already an ordained priest, in the summer of 1950. In 1952 he was appointed Procurator, and Dom Guerric, administrator of Chimay in place of of the stricken Dom Anselm Le Bail, who could not resign because he could not communicate, gave him five years in which to make the Island self-supporting. Chimay, at that time, was having to make good a Caldey financial deficiency of about £4,000 a year.

In the event Caldey was to achieve self-sufficiency and become an Abbey in its own right in 1959. Fr Anthony left the Community to work as a parish priest in 1962.

A man with a great organising ability and business acumen, he had been a bomber pilot at the beginning of the war and then, for much of the time, a prisoner. Contrary to popular belief, although mentioned in dispatches, he received no decorations and was not involved in the Wooden Horse escape from Sagan, but he did spend some time at that camp near Breslau. He does, however, claim to have dug the first escape tunnel for the R.A.F., which was at the transit camp at Dulag Luft from which seventeen escaped. Then he 'joined a digging party' at Barth and 'just went on and on.'

In much of what he did at Caldey he worked closely with Br Thomas, a man with many bright ideas and an ability to involve others, but who was no great administrator. Stories of his forgetfulness are legion. [*Most of them, like so many of the better stories, are apocryphal, but are useful for the more gullible, who are prepared to write their books and their features without the elementary precaution of checking their facts. R.H.*] Br Thomas had much to do with the introduction and building up of the Caldey perfume enterprise, which has now become world famous, and which is of sufficient interest and importance to warrant a chapter to itself later in the book.

Although by 1959 the perfume was making a welcome contribution to the Island's economy, it was not by any means the biggest factor in enabling Caldey to become autonomous, as it did in that year. Up to that time the biggest single cash contribution had come by way of landing fees paid by the daily visitors. Partially, this was due to the increasing holiday trade in the area in those post-war years, but it was also due in no small measure to the greatly improved service offered to holiday-makers by the setting up of the 'Caldey Pool'. Instead of a disorganised free-for-all, it had meant that any visitor to Caldey could buy a ticket on the harbour, covering return boat fare and landing fee, get onto the first avaliable boat, and return on any boat when ready to come back from the Island.

The scheme, inevitably, had its teething troubles, and it was found necessary to prohibit landings by boats other than those operating in the 'Pool'. Amongst other things it also meant the end of occasional boats running trips to Caldey from neigh-bouring Saundersfoot, because anybody taken to Caldey by an outside boat could return on a 'Pool' boat, since no ticket had to be produced for the return journey.

There were internal problems, too. The boatmen decided that the scheme was so well-organised, and that they were in such a strong position, that they could now demand all sorts of improvements to the landing facilities on the Island. On the instructions of the then Prior, Dom Eugene Boylan, Fr Anthony met the boatmen's deputation, gave them a very fair hearing and, when he was satisfied that they had no further points to make, said, 'Very well, gentlemen, the Island is closed as from now.' It took about four days for the boatmen to decide that there were no problems connected with the landing facilities which they could not surmount.

As far as the farming was concerned, there were all the problems which have always faced Island farmers as well as those inherent in the industry itself. However, by the time that autonomy was achieved in 1959, the farm had made, and was still making, only a small contribution to the Community's income. No definite policy was being pursued, and Fr Anthony, with overall responsibility for their financial affairs, but no knowledge of farming, was making a brave attempt to grapple with its many complex problems. Advice was freely sought, and just as freely given, from many quarters, and it was his task to sort it out and follow that which he felt would be of use. He soon came to recognise that some of it was better than others. A gentleman from the National Agricultural Advisory Service suggested they should grow ten acres of cabbages. And the cabbages did well, just as the N.A.A.S. man said they would. And the monks managed to sell some of them, but not many. This nonsense, however, was outside Fr Anthony's control and can more properly be discussed when dealing with other aspects of the Community's life and affairs during those years.

It is, of course, quite ridiculous to plant ten acres of cabbages and then look for a market. The market has to be found before the crop is planted, and then the crop has to be grown in order to supply it. Even without the Island's transport difficulties, such a venture is fraught with danger and financial pitfalls.

I saw something of the monks' farming problems from the inside during those years. Reference has already been made in an earlier chapter to the restrictions on an island farmer's market potential. At this time the comparatively recent introduction of early potatoes as an integral part of the farming system on Pembrokeshire's more favoured coastal farms had become firmly established. Caldey, however, could take no advantage of it. The swing to milk had been accentuated during the war years and Pembrokeshire had become virtually a milk-producing county. Again Caldey could play no part. By this time, too, the post-war betrayal of farmers by the politicians had already started. From 1953 farming returns had been declining steeply. Even on the mainland, beef and sheep producers were faring badly, and milk producers were running into all sorts of problems.

In 1957 I was Chairman of the Pembrokeshire National Farmers' Union County Milk Committee, and Fr Anthony, who had learned enough by this time to appreciates the importance of marketing in the farming business, had asked me whether I could give them any advice on their besetting dairy problems. I would not have presumed to offer advice personally, but I felt that I was in a position to help by arranging for advice to be given by people qualified to give it, and this I did. In the summer of that year I went over to Caldey with Herbert Richards, Willie Uphill and Newton Young. Herbert Richards was the Milk Marketing Board's very experienced Regional Marketing Officer for South Wales, with a complete grasp of the complicated factors involved in the marketing of milk and dairy produce. Willie Uphill was a practical dairy farmer who was Chairman of the Ministry of Agriculture's County Milk Committee, a member of the M.M.B's. South Wales Regional Committee, and with a first-hand knowledge of the Island's farming since he had been going across there as a young man in the 1920's on behalf of the old Pembrokeshire Milk Recording Society. Newton Young was County Secretary of Pembrokeshire N.F.U. and he, too, had considerable knowledge and experience of the milk business. They were all very good friends of mine, it was a glorious day, and made even more memorable for Newton and myself when Fr Anthony and Br Thomas lent us their bathing trunks so that we could go for a swim in the crystal clear, but very cold, waters of Priory Bay, and sat on the quayside giving a gratuitous, and apparently hilarious running commentary on our shivering efforts for the benefit of the two non-swimming members of our deputation.

In the light of more recent developments on the Island farm, which will be referred to later, it will perhaps be relevant and helpful to discuss here in some detail the factors involved in the production and marketing of milk and dairy produce as they affected the thinking of those who were trying to come up with the right answer at that time, coupled as they were with other enterprises on the Island.

Because of the transport costs and problems it was out of the question to think of concentrating solely on beef and fat lamb production, even if they had been profitable. For the same reasons potatoes could not be considered, and the selling of liquid milk to the creameries was also not possible. Yet at that time milk was more profitable than anything else, mainly because of the stability brought about by the Milk Marketing

Board, and Fr Anthony was keen to explore all the possibilities, because farming remains a part of the Cistercians' way of life.

Under the Agriculture Act of 1947 there was a guaranteed price for a certain agreed quantity of milk produced by farmers in a year, and this was known as the standard quantity. By 1957 the system was seen to be not nearly as helpful or advantageous as had been suggested when the Act was introduced. The standard quantity was about the same as the quantity of milk which could be sold on the liquid market. This milk earned the top price. Anything over and above this went for manufacture, mainly into butter and cheese, and earned a much lower price because of the competition from cheap, subsidised imports, often dumped here by other countries, to get rid of their own surpluses, at completely unrealistic prices. The average of the total earnings, from milk sold liquid and from milk sold for manufacture, was known as the 'pool price', and this determined the price per gallon which the milk producer finally received for all the milk he sold. It followed that the more milk that was sold for manufacture, the lower was the pool price. And, by 1957, the farming industry had answered the national plea for increased production to such an extent that far more milk was being produced than was needed to supply the liquid market, so that all the excess milk going for manufacture was losing money and depressing the price still further. At that time the price fixed for the standard quantity, as being fair and necessary for the farmer to earn a reasonable living, was about three shillings and sixpence a gallon. But the milk which went for manufacture was earning only one and eightpence a gallon, so that on this milk alone the farmer was losing nearly two shillings a gallon, whilst it depressed the overall pool price to three shillings a gallon. And this actual return was one which, it was admitted by Government, was not enough.

It would have needed the wisdom of Solomon to show the monks how to make any money from milk in such a situation. They had tried making cream without any marked success, and Fr Anthony hoped that butter might have proved a more practical possibility. It would have meant producing milk which would have earned, through manufacture, only a fraction of what it could have earned on the liquid market, even if the monks could have had access to such a market. The hope that the butter could have been marketed at a special premium was a forlorn one, for much of the butter with which it would have had to compete was being sold under all sorts of fancy names and trade marks implying that it was the produce of the rich pastures of Welsh lowland farms, but carrying in tiny print on the back, where no-one was likely to see it, the words 'including imported butter'. This meant that about ninety-five percent of it would have come from abroad, whilst those who were responsible were enabled to describe themselves, somewhat euphemistically, as butter blenders.

At that time there were about twenty-five cows on the Island. Some of these were Dairy Shorthorns, descendants of those which were there when the monks came to Caldey, but a policy had been embarked upon of going in for Jerseys, renowned for the high butterfat content of their milk, and the herd had become one in which the cows of this breed predominated. Their milk was ideal, and something of a luxury, for supplying the needs of the monks and the inhabitants of the eighteen houses on the Island. Fr Anthony was mainly concerned with disposing of whatever milk was surplus to these requirements. The perfume industry seemed to be progressing on sound lines and he wanted to do the same for the farm, but he did not want to embark on building up the much bigger herd which would have been essential to justify the installation of the equipment necessary to a manufacturing enterprise. There had been big changes since the time, thirty years previously, when there had been fifty cows on Caldey and butter-making was still the order of the day on many mainland farms. With some sort of order having been brought to the marketing of fresh milk, in spite of the persistent attempts by politicians to sabotage the good work, that was now considerably more attractive than making butter. But such an enterprise would have been no sinecure in the 1950's. Furthermore, there was no way of disposing of the skim milk left behind when milk is separated for the cream to be made into butter. It is highly suitable for feeding to pigs but, at that time, the idea of a herd of pigs on Caldey was still only an idea.

The only possible solution at that time, particularly as the main requirement was merely to find an outlet for the surplus milk, was to have most of the cows calving in the spring, so that they would be in full production during the summer months, and to sell as much milk as possible as an attractive beverage to the ever-increasing, and now much better organised, daily visitors. Thus was born the milk-bar in the Island's tea-rooms, and the Milk Marketing Board provided the equipment. It was no long-term solution to any problem, but explains what was happening at that time, and makes more easily understandable the farming programme which subsequently developed.

11
THE PERFUME INDUSTRY

'Ointment and perfume rejoice the heart': Proverbs 27:9

In the many articles which have been written about the Caldey monks during recent years, the idea has often been expressed or implied that there is somehow something incongruous about such unworldly characters as monks being engaged in making something as worldly, frivolous and feminine as perfume. To think on these lines, however, is to be unmindful of the fact that perfume has a long history of religious association, and there is reference to it in this respect very early in the Old Testament. Indeed, the word itself, taken from the Latin *per fumum*, means simply 'from smoke'. The first perfumes, used to counteract the offensive smells from burning flesh in religious sacrifices, were obtained by the combustion of aromatic woods and gums.

There was, however, no religious background to the introduction of perfume manufacture to Caldey, nor can the establishment of this very successful enterprise be attributed to any one person or single happening. It evolved as a result of a number of things happening at the same time.

If there was any definite starting point, it was perhaps in those critical financial years after the war when the survival of the Community was in jeopardy, and they were all trying desperately to think up ideas for making things to sell to the day-visitors. Br Stanislaus, a very knowledgeable botanist and horticulturist, came up with the idea, as his contribution, of selling bunches of dried herbs and everlasting flowers. Br Stanislaus was given the idea by Br Teilo, a 'very loveable' old oblate who had been on Caldey with the Benedictines and remained on the Island when the Cistercians came. In earlier years he had been a tram driver in Newport in the days of the old horse-drawn trams. He had sold bunches of lavender with the Benedictines, and now passed on the idea to Br Stanislaus in the Cistercians' financial extremity. They were beautifully done up in ribbon, and scented with perfume obtained from

Miss Harrison, a clever perfumer, who had retired to live in one
of the Island cottages and who made beautiful perfume from
rosemary and roses. She promised to give the monks her
recipe, but eventually died without having done so.

It was a time when people had been starved of many luxuries,
and they snapped up eagerly the beautiful little novelties which
Br Stanislaus created for their delight. The demand for them
was so enthusiastic that Br Thomas offered the thought that it
might be possible to make lavender water from the lavender
growing on the Island. From there on they travelled many a
blind mile on the way to the eventual success that the venture
was destined to become.

The only lavender Br Stanislaus had was the Old English
variety, which grew very tall, but was too 'harsh' to be of any
use for perfume, although it would serve for sachets. Br
Thomas was put in touch with Fr Damian, an Augustinian
Friar, who had a factory in AniVres, which had been started to
provide work for the unemployed. Eventually Br Thomas went
over to Paris to discuss his ideas in more detail, and Fr Damian
then came to Caldey to help make the first batch of lavender
perfume. Because of the unsuitability of the Island lavender for
the purpose, it was made with a bought essence but, unfortunately, because nothing was known of the U.K. alcohol regulations,
it was made with industrial methylated spirits, and gallons of
the finished product were of no use. Br Thomas persevered,
however, and the first perfume was sold on the Island in 1953.
The enterprise was on a very small scale, with the village
helpers bottling the product with pipettes, but it was a
beginning and, like the bunches of dried flowers, shrubs and
herbs, the perfume was bought eagerly.

At that time consideration was also being given to the
possibility of starting an industry which would be sufficiently
flexible to allow time for the following of the monastic vocation.
It had long been apparent that the farm alone would not be able
to support the Community, and the day-visitor trade had not
then developed to the same extent as in later years. One idea
being considered was carpet-making, but it was eventually
abandoned because the people who were going to teach the
monks the craft wanted a share in the business and, in any case,

the necessary machinery would have required considerable capital outlay.

The idea of a perfume enterprise seemed to be much more worth pursuing. It required no heavy outlay for machinery and, in so many ways, met the requirements for overcoming the problems inherent in island production and marketing. Perfume would have a high value-to-weight ratio, would be easy to store, and easy to transport. Much of it, by way of a bonus, could be sold on the Island at the retail price, without needing to be transported to the mainland.

Dom Albert Derzelle and Fr Anthony went to London to ask Henry Kobus, a young Polish pharmacist and perfumer, to come to Caldey to help them. It needed more than one visit to persuade him, but he was a Catholic and well-disposed towards the Community, and eventually he agreed to come, arriving in the December of 1953.

He began work in the kitchen of one of the cottages with cups, saucers and glasses. Whilst waiting to obtain the different raw materials, which takes a long time, and being keen to produce something by the time the first of the season's visitors arrived, he made a hand lotion with natural materials found in a chemist's shop on the mainland. Although it was meant only as a stop-gap, it developed into one of the best selling lines, which is perhaps understandable because, being made with natural ingredients, it is one of the best hand lotions on the market.

Initially, of course, the idea was to make perfume from those shrubs and herbs which already grew, or could be grown, on the Island. Henry Kobus, therefore, went to the monastery at Aiguebelle in the south of France where they had large lavender plantations, and brought back new varieties of lavender grown in the south of France in the regions of Drôme and the Maritime Alps, to see which would do best on Caldey and produce the right oil. Another shrub introduced at that time was *Lippia Citrodora* known also as Aloysia or Lemon Verbena, the only plant from which true verbane oil is derived and, although of the same species, not to be confused with the *verbena officinalis* or vervain.

Vervain was the sacred herb of the ancient Druids and amongst the plants dedicated to the service of the altar and the decoration of the priesthood. In ancient Greece the plant was believed to possess great virtues, and the Romans usually offered it as a pledge of good faith to their enemies. The Anglo-Saxons wore it as a good-luck charm to keep away the Devil and to ward off the disease of scrofula. Whilst this plant, however, will grow almost anywhere, the lemon verbena is much less hardy and can only be grown so successfully on Caldey because of the Island's temperate climate.

As the perfume industry grew, it was found necessary to purchase more and more of the essential oils, until the lavender and lemon verbena were discontinued as sources of oil for the perfume and toilet water and are now used only in pot pourri.

Of even more significance was the use of a plant or small shrub, as common on Caldey as anywhere else, known variously as gorse, furze or whin, the bloom of which turns banks and hillsides to a glorious yellow from spring to summer. In other days the young, prickly shoots were crushed and fed to cattle and horses, the stalks were used for heating the old bread ovens, and the bark is still used in parts of Scotland for a yellow dye in the manufacture of tartan cloth. The blossom is also used for the making of a sweet golden coloured wine. Augustus John, the artist who was born in Tenby, is reputed to have named it 'Gorse Champagne'.

These uses apart, gorse is not a plant which man has ever much encouraged, regarding it for the most part as something of a nuisance. For many years perfumers tried, without success, to extract oil from the gorse bloom. Henry Kobus persisted with this idea and carried out experiments with Professor Sabetay in Paris, who was very interested in the possibilities. The essential oil, obtained from gorse flowers by alcoholic extraction, has a very delicate odour, clean and fresh, with a sweet undertone. The experiments eventually met with success, and Caldey became the only perfumery in the world to utilise gorse in this way, using it for perfume and sachets.

The business once begun, the first venture onto the mainland to promote the new product came in the summer of 1956 with a little exhibit at the Bath and West Show in Cardiff. Br Thomas, as usual, was very enthusiastic, and I did a short radio broadcast on it. It was the first broadcast on something which has since received a fair measure of coverage on television and radio, and in the press. In spite of his enthusiasm, however, I remember, too, sensing a note of apprehension in Br Thomas's conversation. Fr Anthony was with him. Eventually, when I had talked about the possibility of success, Br Thomas looked at Fr Anthony, then at me, and as they exchanged a wry smile, said, 'If it isn't a success, then I shall be for the high jump.' I did not at that time appreciate what he was trying to say, but it should be self-evident in the next chapter.

For all the mistaken notions which outsiders may hold, Caldey is not without its romantic moments. [*Those who have not already done so might care to read the last chapter of my book Caldey—R.H.*]. Henry Kobus met the sister of one of the monks, Br James, there and married her. With the prospect of their children having to start school, they followed a pattern all too familiar to island people and decided on a return to the mainland. That was in 1959, the year in which Caldey became self-supporting. Although the perfume industry by that time had been established on sound lines, it will be seen that it had not achieved sufficient success to be making anything like a major contribution to the monastery's income. That success was to come later.

The 'brain' from there on became Walter Poucher, world-famous perfumer, whose books on the subject are standard works. He agreed, in his retirement, to act as a consultant for a fee of one hundred guineas a visit. In the event he became so charmed with the Island and the Community that he refused to accept payment. He introduced a number of new lines and, in the next decade, helped to build up the business to one which now turns out perfume of world class. Caldey perfume is not merely a novelty because it is made by monks. Because they do not price their own labour very highly, and especially by cutting out the middle men by selling direct to the customer, they are able to support old-fashioned hand methods, which would spell financial ruin for more modern enterprises, and offer products which, in today's conveyor-belt economy, are unique.

Many of the essential raw materials are now imported from all over the world, and the bottles and packaging are made to order. Four monks are employed in the manufacture, with the help of Islanders at odd times. Not least of the advantages of the enterprise is that, apart from any economic considerations, it is sufficiently flexible to allow those involved to follow their monastic vocation and, additionally, be busy at the work during the winter, ready to sell to the visitors in the summer.

12
CHANGES IN LEADERSHIP

'Every man hath his proper gift of God, one after this manner, and another after that': Corinthians 7:7

It has been seen from earlier chapters that, because of the fulness of the monks' daily lives, coupled with their vow of obedience, a very great responsibility devolves upon the Superior. This part of the Community's life from the end of the war to the achievement of full autonomy in 1959 was as full of problems as those aspects dealt with in the preceding chapters. No fewer than five men were involved, each being great in his own way.

To write fairly and with authority on the men who virtually controlled the Community's destiny, during those fourteen or fifteen difficult years, is perhaps the most hazardous part of a work such as this, especially for someone outside the Community, because it involves making an assessment. This is something which can only be done after talking to people involved and they cannot be quoted. Not least of the many deeply gratifying feelings in writing this book has been to experience the degree of trust which so many people have shown in being willing to speak freely on confidential matters. In any Community or family there are bound to be little irritations and personal frictions. Whilst monks are seeking to attain perfection, they make no claim to having achieved it, and they are only human. Different people will react in different ways towards others and they will take differing views of different happenings. A very good monk in pursuit of union with God may be very happy and willing to give of his utmost in physical labour, without having the faintest idea of the commercial value of the end product. Equally, a good man in every sense of the word, with that keen business sense needed to make it possible for the Community to pay its way and stay together to observe the Holy Rule of St Benedict, may not himself be a particularly good monk when it comes to the observance of that Rule. Each man's opinion, therefore, however sincere and honest it may be, will be influenced according to his own effort and beliefs. Having talked to many, I can only, in my own turn, and for what it may be worth, write of the situation and the events as I have understood them.

Fr Jerome took over, with great humility, as a temporary measure when Fr Odo, and then Fr Aelred Lefevre, died within weeks of each other. When a successor had been appointed, Fr Jerome returned to Chimay very weary from all the many responsibilities he had been carrying. It was not long, however, before he was back on Caldey, and he continued to give wonderful service to the Community until his death in 1974.

Some reference has already been made in a previous chapter to the fine qualities of Dom Albert Derzelle, the Belgian, who was appointed Prior of Caldey by Chimay in 1946 and was subsequently elected by the Community. He was not a great business man, but he was a saintly man, and a great spiritual leader. And this was the need of the Community at that time. The intake of novices was spectacular and it inspired new hope. But we have seen, too, the desperate financial problems of those years, and the effect on him can be imagined. Perhaps the terrible worry of financial cares can never be so great as for those who, by nature, are ill-equipped to cope with them, and it must have been greatly distressing to have had the threat of closure constantly hanging over his head. His great spiritual achievements, therefore, become even more remarkable when they are seen against the background of such constant anxiety, aggravated as always by the very fact of having to live and earn a living on an island. There were times when they had barely enough money in the bank to live for a week. To borrow was not part of their way of life and, in any case, would have been no answer in the long term.

It is not to be wondered at that Dom Albert's health suffered and, mentally and physically exhausted, he resigned in the autumn of 1954 and returned to Chimay. After a few years, and when his health had improved, he went out to the Congo as a monk and subsequently became Prior of the Monastery there.

During Dom Albert's illness, a great Frenchman, Dom Godefroid Belorgey, had come to take charge. From references to him in the Journal extracts it will have been seen that he had been very highly placed in the Cistercian Order. Originally

Novice Master at Chimay, he had become Auxiliary Abbot at Citeaux, second only to the Abbot General of the Order, and had presided there for more than twenty years. Some of the older French and Belgian monks at Caldey had been his novices in their early years at Chimay and, understandably, they revered him. But he was now an old man and spoke very little English. Equally understandably, therefore, the younger Brothers (predominantly English-speaking) were less enthusiastic, and much of the good work done by Dom Albert in attracting these much-needed recruits could have been put in jeopardy.

There were further difficulties and complications. Dom Guerric, it will be remembered, was acting Superior at Chimay in the final years of Dom Anselm Le Bail's fatal illness following his stroke and total paralysis. Dom Guerric was Abbot in everything except name. Yet, although he could give Fr Anthony five years to make the Island pay under threat of closure, he could not, under canon law, carry out the Visitation. This was undertaken by Dom Columban Mulcahy, the Irish Abbot of the monastery at Nunraw in Scotland, a foundation of Roscrea, who, not surprisingly perhaps, insisted on the appointment of an English-speaking Prior. This it was which partially precipitated the resignation of Dom Albert and led, in the autumn of 1954, to the recall from an Australian monastery of Dom Eugene Boylan, who had been sent there from the Irish Abbey at Roscrea to found a monastery near Melbourne.

There is a fairly general belief outside Caldey that Dom Eugene was a hand-picked man, sent there because of his great business acumen, to sort out the Island's financial troubles, and that he succeeded in doing this. It is also thought that, because he was a nuclear physicist, he was responsible for developing the perfume industry. He may have encouraged the perfume developments, but no more, for he had no great aptitude for business.

He came to Caldey as Prior when he did because the Community asked for him. The need for an English-speaking Prior had already been established but, amongst their own number, the English-speaking Brothers were all young, without the experience to qualify them for taking on such an onerous task. In 1950 Dom Eugene had come to Caldey to preach a Retreat and had made a deep impression on the Community. This is understandable, for he was a man with a marvellous brain and tremendous ability. He had studied nuclear physics at Vienna, had taught philosophy and theology at Mount St Joseph College, Roscrea, and had lectured in physics at Dublin University. A well-known author on the spiritual life, he had translated into English Dom Godefroid Belorgey's book, *The Practice of Mental Prayer*. For good measure, he was a brilliant musician, and could discourse knowledgeably and fluently on virtually any subject anyone wanted to discuss.

Unfortunately, he could not delegate responsibility, and seemed almost to resent any monk getting on with his allotted job with the degree of initiative advocated by Dom Anselm Le Bail during his Visitation, as recorded in the Journal, twenty years earlier. Without having any business sense, he was always ready to interfere and start up all kinds of ill-thought out schemes advocated by all sorts of people. The growing of ten acres of cabbages referred to earlier was just one example. There was a complete lack of co-ordination, and I sensed something of this during my own contacts in 1957 without at that time understanding the cause. Although complete autonomy was achieved as a result of financial independence in 1959, it did not come because of Dom Eugene. To others must go the credit for making this achievement possible.

One monk, perhaps, put it as well as anybody in talking of Dom Eugene, when he said, 'It was simply a case of not perhaps the right man in the right place at the right time.' And the monk who said that thought highly of him because he believed he had a marvellous understanding of men with spiritual problems. Full of compassion, he was a great man spiritually, and this was important to the men with all sorts of problems and mixed-up thinking in those post-war years. As a second-in-command, with this sort of responsibility, he could have done great work and achieved much. It was no fault of his that he was not a born leader.

When, in 1959, Caldey became an Abbey in its own right, the Community democratically elected one of their own Brothers, James Wicksteed, as their first Abbot. He was thirty-eight at the time, and was one of the four novices who had been sent to Chimay and subsequently recalled.

The Irish monks seemed to think that Don Eugene had not been fully appreciated. They gained the impression, however, that it had come as a relief to him not to have been chosen as Abbot. He said to one of them, 'The big problem was that my mother had bought a new hat in readiness for the occasion' —which seems to suggest that he took it in the right spirit. And this indeed is the truth of the matter, because he was undeniably very disappointed, but demonstrated that, if he did have some shortcomings, he was a 'big' man.

Following this he returned to his own Abbey at Roscrea and was subsequently elected Abbot. The tragic news of his death in a car not long afterwards came as no surprise to those who knew him, for the mainland stories of his Jehu-like driving were as legendary as those [*mostly apocryphal*] of Brother Thomas's forgetfulness, and ready wit [*fact*].

Dom James Wicksteed was born to parents who were Shakespearian actors. Because of the uncertainty of this way of life he decided on a monastic vocation. A novice at the Benedictine Monastery at Belmont at the outbreak of war, he joined the R.A.F. and served throughout the war. He may not have realised it at the time, but he gained some useful experience for his future responsibilities by being involved in clearing up at Belsen concentration camp after the liberation. After the war he joined the Benedictines at Prinknash. The life, however, did not seem to provide him with the answer for which he was seeking, and he came to Caldey as a Cistercian novice in 1949.

[*After serving for twenty-one years as Abbot, Dom James Wicksteed resigned in 1980 and left Caldey to involve himself in charitable work. He was succeeded by Dom Robert O'Brien, who for some time had been serving as Prior, and who thus became Caldey's second Abbot.*]

When Dom James Wicksteed became Caldey's first Abbot, the challenge facing the Community was different from anything they had experienced previously. It is not unknown for people to turn to God in time of trouble. And the monks had experienced plenty of that. But it is perhaps an even greater challenge to true monasticism, when men seek union with God—trying to be poor with the poor Christ—when their state is one of financial security. Jesus knew what he was talking about when He talked to His disciples of the challenge of the rich man entering the Kingdom of Heaven.

As we saw in an earlier chapter, there is democracy in a monastic community, and decisions can be reached on a community basis. But this is not the complete answer. It is the Abbot who, in the final event, has to take the big decisions. He stands as God's deputy and there is obedience to him.

As Donald Hayne wrote in his autobiography, *Batter My Heart*, 'In a religious Order, obedience and conformity are virtues freely undertaken by more or less mature men and women with the definite object, held consciously in view, of voluntarily subjecting their individual judgement and preferences to the common work of their institute and the will of their superiors seen supernaturally as expressing the will of God.'

Overall, the Abbot has two tremendous responsibilities. He has to ensure financial viability. Although money surplus to the needs of the Community is all given away, the making of money for this purpose is not the main objective. If a monk were to see this as his function in life he might just as well join a Community as a teacher or healer, or even become a priest. Above all, he must still pursue his monastic calling. The balance between the two responsibilities is bound to create problems, especially in an area such as that in which Caldey is situated, with heavy seasonal demands upon time and labour.

From here on the story of Caldey is largely about the way in which the problem has been tackled and an attempt made to reconcile these two vital issues.

13
PIGS AND POULTRY

'One generation passeth away, and another generation cometh:
but the earth abideth for ever': Ecclesiastes 1:4

For various reasons it was a long time before the farming on Caldey was able to reach as high a standard as the Cistercian monks, traditional farmers, would have wished. In their first decade there they had experienced the fearful depression of the times. Then had come the war years with a crippling shortage of man-power. Overall was the additional problem of almost every operation being that much more difficult for the island farmer who has always been restricted in the lines of production available to him.

After the war came the concerted effort to which reference has already been made. High on the list of priorities, as can be imagined, was the rebuilding of the church which had been burned down during the war. This took place in the early 1950's with the monks doing much of the work themselves, helped by monks from other monasteries. The choir stalls were made for them in Belgium, from wood known as *Wenge* and grown in the Congo, where Chimay has a daughter house.

Communication with the mainland was improved when, for the first time since the severing of the telephone cable in 1938, a radio telephone was installed in 1951. The kiosk installed in the village was the first in the United Kingdom to be connected by radio link. Then, in 1958, a start was made towards improving landing facilities for the boats.

Three barges, which had been intended for use in the D-Day invasion, but had not been used, were towed across the bay from Burry Port and filled with concrete in order to sink them and extend the quay. This work has been added to over the years, widening and improving the quay.

With winches on the quaysides at Tenby and on the Island, and the purchase of an old lorry for use on the Island, a mechanised system of handling goods in large crates was introduced and this, like the restoration of the telephone and the improvements to the quay, made a contribution towards a more efficient farming programme. In so far, that is, as the farming of an island can ever be efficient.

Mention has already been made of the possibilities which had been considered for a dairy enterprise in 1957, and of the factors which had limited them. It was therefore decided instead to restrict milk production to as much as was required for the Community, and for use in the tea room, to build up pig and poultry enterprises, and to increase the flock of sheep. In many ways it was good thinking and, for a time, served well enough.

As far as the sheep and pigs were concerned, it meant, very broadly, fattening the lambs off grass and the pigs off the Island's corn. To this end the arable acreage was increased and about 160 acres of barley were being grown for feeding to the sixty sows and their progeny. Because of the problems of transport, the beef cattle were phased out, since they were very much more difficult to handle than fat lambs, and the milking cows were kept to a minimum. For the most part, therefore, the grass acreage was geared to the needs of the sheep, whilst they, in turn, with their traditional 'golden hoof', built up the fertility of the land. When the grassland was ploughed, after a few years of being grazed by sheep, good yields of barley were assured.

With barley readily available on the Island, the pigs developed into a considerable enterprise, and the Caldey herd of pedigree Large White sows became very well-known, as did the Caldey pork. In fact, the Caldey pork was so well-known that the pork in one mainland butcher's shop was still being sold as Caldey-produced two years after the monks had ceased to keep pigs!

In addition to the fattening of some of the progeny for pork or bacon,. there were also useful sales of some of the better boars and gilts as breeding stock. In order to find a 'shop-window' for this class of stock, a certain amount of exhibiting at shows was undertaken, and the monks in charge of the pigs became familiar figures with their Large Whites at many of the agricultural shows on the mainland during the summer.

Since the war, however, there has also been considerable emphasis on performance, as well as pedigree and looks, in all classes of stock. In the case of pigs, performance has been judged on the number of piglets born to a sow in each litter, the number reared successfully, the rate at which they have grown, and the weight and quality of meat they have produced when slaughtered. Some of these figures were produced at the Pig Industry Development Authority, as it then was, at Corsham in Wiltshire. Four pigs from a litter had to be taken to Corsham. They would be two boars, a hog and a gilt. The hog and the gilt would be slaughtered at bacon weight, and the boars, provided they had reached satisfactory standards, could then be brought back onto the farm and sold for stock purposes. It involved a great deal of work, and also travelling, for anyone situated as far away from Corsham as Pembrokeshire is. For the monks, there was all this, plus the problem of transport from Tenby to Caldey at the end of the journey. Occasionally, arrangements had to be made to leave the pigs on mainland farms until the weather was suitable for the crossing to be made.

It was an era when farming techniques were becoming increasingly sophisticated, and all these things had to be done if the monks were to be able to stay in business in competition with the best. To make pigs pay they had to exploit them to the full and this was the only way to do it.

The demand for pedigree breeding stock, however, would vary according to the profitability of pigs at any particular time. And the variability of the pig trade has always been notorious, showing a graph with a consistent pattern of peaks and toughs. The reason is not far to seek. A gilt, as a young sow is called, will produce her first litter when she is a year old, and thereafter will have two litters par year. Assuming half of these are gilts, it will be seen that it is possible to increase the number of sows in a herd very quickly, unlike cattle which normally have one calf a year, or sheep which have one or two lambs a year. As soon as pigs become unprofitable, many farmers, quite naturally, give up keeping them. In the period of shortage which follows, better prices result and farmers are tempted to start keeping them again. Because the sow herd can be built up so quickly, the demand is soon supplied and is followed by another slump.

However useful the sale of breeding stock was in the Caldey pig business, most of the income was from the sale of the progeny, which had been reared for slaughter, either as pork or as bacon, according to which would be more profitable at the time. Like other pig-keepers, the monks had their good times and they had their bad times. And, like other pig-keepers, they had to work out for themselves whether the good times were good enough to make it worthwhile hanging on when times were bad and until good times came round again.

The Island at this time was a busy place, with all the outward signs of prosperity. There were the improved landing facilities. In the early 1960's work was begun on making a concrete road all the way from the quay up to the farm, and finally into the kitchen gardens. In 1965 there was an event of great moment when a mains electricity cable was laid to replace the diesel-powered Island generators. A submarine cable had already been installed to replace the radio telephone. The coming of mains electricity meant a reduction in the quantity of diesel fuel which had to be manhandled, and it meant the end of the annual slog involved in taking delivery of more than a hundred tons of coal.

As far as the pigs were concerned, it meant the benefit of infra-red rearing lamps, which previously had been severely restricted. But with sixty sows, and therefore anything up to five hundred pigs on the Island at any one time, the problems of the bad years were considerable. Once again it was the old, old story. No matter how slender the margin of profit, the monks had to bear the extra costs of crossing to the mainland, with all the attendant handling, so that the good years could never be good enough to see them through the bad years. There is no need to ask, therefore, why it was finally decided that pig production was not the right answer, and the decision was taken to think along other lines.

The abandonment of another project, the very considerable poultry fattening enterprise, was even more understandable. There has probably been a greater revolution in this branch of farming than in any other since the war. Indeed, it is doubtful whether poultry can any longer be regarded as part of the true agricultural pattern, and the trends have given rise to the term 'factory farming'. The monks went into this line of production when people still tended to think of poultry as creatures of the farm and, at one time, they were producing 15,000 birds a year. The system is intensive, the competition keen, and the margin per bird very slight. Profitability depends on sufficient birds coming out of 'the factory'. Unlike the pigs, which were fed chiefly on barley grown on the Island, the poultry were kept on feed which had to be imported. Competitors supplying mainland shops, at prices which transformed poultry from a luxury into staple diet, had no such expenses to meet, either in getting the feed to the point where it was needed, or in getting the final product back across the water. It was all a far cry from the system when Br James used to remove the eggs from the gulls' cliff-top nests and replace them with goose eggs for the gulls to incubate and hatch out the young goslings. The modern poultry venture, therefore, lasted only a short time.

So, then, for all the careful thought and planning, and for all the investment and energy and the hard work involved, the farming on Caldey brought in no more than the modest returns of such farms on the mainland. A typical magazine feature of the period, written by someone who went no deeper than the surface, and who knew nothing of farming, referred to 'evidence of wealth, tractors, machinery and the technical gadgets of a complete 20th century existence,' without realising that these things are the price which has to be paid by those who farm. They have very often hardly paid for themselves by the time they need to be replaced. On the mainland, farmers can spread the cost of this machinery by taking on more land, if and when it is available. It has meant a constantly changing idea of what is now thought of as a small farm. When the monks came to Caldey, a farm of thirty acres was a useful holding capable of supporting a young family. Today, a hundred-acre farm is no more than a small-holding.

To understand something of these matters is to realise why the farm on Caldey could not now come anywhere near to supporting the Island's Community in the absence of any other source of income.

14
TENBY HARBOUR AND DISPUTATIONS

Better is a little with righteousness than great revenues without right': Proverbs 16:8

Municipal Authorities are traditional targets for the strictures of critics, and butts for the wit of comedians and lampooners, as well as being the despair of the long-suffering ratepayers. The picture, of course, is never quite what it seems, and the background facts are not always known and understood. Even so, when all due allowances have been made, history will not be hard put to it to find examples of greater collective wisdom than that evinced by the Tenby Borough Council from time time to time during the 1950's and '60's.

As it affected Caldey, difficulty possibly began in the late 1940's with a suggestion to pull down the Royal Victoria Pier which had been built by the Borough Council, with some private financial aid, between 1897 and 1899. The Borough Council had spent little by way of maintenance over the years on this most useful amenity, and in the post-war years were faced with the need to carry out certain repair work.

It was an era when councillors had not yet begun to realise that they were merely tools in the hands of central government, and genuinely believed that, by their own action, or lack of it, they could could keep down the rates. It became the rule in the ancient borough to spend nothing. A noisy, but influential, minority bludgeoned their fellow members into acquiescing with the idea that everything with which they were concerned should produce revenue.

In the post-war years, P. & A. Campbell had proposed restarting their paddle steamer pleasure cruises from Tenby, which had been so popular before the war. The Borough Council, however, were advised that certain repair work would be necessary before the Victoria Pier could again be used for this purpose. Negotiations with people who expressed an interest in purchasing the Pier came to nothing and, in March 1951, the Town Clerk wrote to Campbells informing them that the Council had entered into a contract to carry out repairs. The cost would be £8,000. After work had commenced, the consulting engineers advised that the work would probably cost another £9,000, and the keepers of the municipal purse decided, in the face of much criticism, that it would be better business to pull the Pier down than to do any more repairs.

Experts are all right, of course, apart from the fact that they are so often wrong. Even where they are not wrong, other experts can be found to disagree with them. In the event, the Pier was found to be in much better shape than the experts had predicted, and the decision to demolish it was seen for what many had always said it was, an act of monumental folly.

It is difficult to obtain exact figures on the destruction (the word is used advisedly) of the Royal Victoria Pier, because the business was very protracted. The firm engaged eventually went into voluntary liquidation, and explosives had to be used before the job was completed four years later.

The same mentality was brought to bear upon the management of the Harbour, with little apparent understanding of the attraction it had for the summer visitors who brought so much money into the town. Small wonder that such an asset to the holiday trade of off-shore Caldey seemed to be completely unappreciated by the same small minority.

In all fairness, the point should be made that few people at that time could have envisaged the huge increase in the summer holiday trade which was about to take place, or foresee the need for facilities for more and bigger boats.

Wisely or foolishly, according to the individual point-of-view, by the early 1960's the Borough Council had reached a stage when a series of events culminated in the need to appoint a new Town Clerk, and there was not a single applicant for the post. Mr Wynne Samuel, a barrister who had tried for a short time without any conspicuous success to practise on the Swansea circuit, was appointed.

So much, then, for the background to what was to happen concerning Tenby Harbour, as it affected the Caldey Community, for the better part of two decades. At the risk of becoming tedious certain of the facts have to be spelled out in more detail.

Back in 1931 the monks had obtained permission from the Borough Council to put a crane on the Harbour. One of the conditions with which they had to comply, and indeed were more than happy to do so, was that the crane should be available for the use of any other of the Harbour users. It was especially useful for lifting engines out of the boats in the autumn and putting them in again in the spring. The crane was damaged in 1938 when being used by one of the Tenby boatmen and could not be replaced until 1946. The correspondence concerning this at the time of its installation in 1931 shows clearly that, in spite of all that was happening at the time, as related in an earlier chapter, there was immense goodwill on the part of the Borough Council towards the monks. Similarily, when the opportunity came to replace it in 1946, the courteous and friendly letters from the Town Clerk at that time showed that the same goodwill was still much in evidence. In 1951 there was a letter from the Town Clerk thanking the monks for their great help in the use of their crane in the handling of timbers in conjunction with work on the Victoria Pier.

By the late 1950's there was correspondence on the need to make the Harbour pay. The Victoria Pier was shown in the Harbour accounts, and it was now being suggested, therefore, that the cost of demolishing this great amenity to the holiday town should be met by the Harbour users, through revenue raised from charges on their activities.

It is odd to reflect, in situations such as that which now developed, how a handful of people can cause sufficient agitation to give an entirely wrong impression. By this time the people of Tenby generally were most kindly disposed towards the monks, as were the majority of the Borough councillors. Yet the whole nonsense which developed was allowed to drag on for more than another decade.

Following the recognition in 1957 that any appreciable expansion of the dairy enterprise on Caldey was not at that time the answer to the Island's agricultural problems, the poultry unit, as related earlier, was introduced and expanded. It was a time when there was a hopeless misunderstanding of agricultural affairs, as there invariably is, by those who do not live by the land. The situation was much aggravated by the system of spending millions of pounds on subsidies which, directly and indirectly, kept down to an artificial level the price which consumers had to pay for the food they ate, whilst the idea was constantly nurtured by politicians that these subsidies were for the benefit of the farmers. The nation consequently thought it was treating its farmers very well and that farmers were making a wonderful living. There was no reason to expect the Tenby Borough councillors to be any wiser than anybody else, and, in answer to the vociferous demands of the minority that the Harbour should be regarded as a source of revenue, it was decided to make a *per capita* charge on everything which the monks shipped through the Harbour. One example was the proposed charge of sixpence on every chicken. This was subsequently reduced to fourpence.

By 1959 the Borough Council had asked for a Public Enquiry and, on July 2nd of that year, the solicitors to the Community wrote to the then Town Clerk of Tenby saying, amongst other things:

On the 5th of September, 1957, we wrote to one of your pre-decessors asking for information on nine specific matters. For your convenience we enclose a copy of our letter.

We have not been given the information for which we then asked. We repeat our request and shall be obliged if you will now give us this information.

Will you please also now supply us with the information for which we asked in our letter of the 1st September (copy enclosed)? This was refused by the Borough Accountant in his letter of the 6th September, 1958, but, in a letter, dated the 11th September, 1958, the Borough Accountant, whilst persisting in his refusal, stated that, should there be an Inquiry, he would endeavour to answer any permissible questions that might be put to him. In view of the fact that an Inquiry has been ordered we repeat our request and ask that the information be given to us forthwith.

The letter then went on to deal with points concerning the inclusion of 'Loan Charges' in connection with the Victoria Pier, and asking for details of these charges and for replies to certain other letters.

Acting for the monks at that time, in day-to-day contact with the Council and the people of Tenby, were Br Thomas, as Island Steward, and Fr Anthony, as Procurator.

The Enquiry was held in July 1959, and received full press coverage locally. The National Farmers' Union supported the monks.

The case having been put for the Council, including the fact that the monks paid no rates on the Island, the Borough Treasurer, Mr M.B. Eastlake, gave a list of suggested improvements, one of which would be the provision of a crane for the use of all persons in the Harbour as the present crane was the property of the monks and was used almost exclusively by them. (This is worth noting and remembering.)

The monks were represented by Mr F.Elwyn Jones, Q.C., and certain passages of the report from *The Tenby Observer* are perhaps worth quoting:

> In reply to Mr Elwyn Jones, Mr Eastlake agreed that the Harbour was a source of natural attraction to visitors to Tenby. He also agreed that the Caldey Community and monastery were a considerable source of attraction. It was the most popular trip in Tenby and one of the things that brought visitors to the town.
>
> Mr Elwyn Jones asked Mr Eastlake if there was any hostility towards the Caldey Community.
>
> 'I am on the most friendly terms with them,' he replied.
>
> 'Do you consider it a reasonable proposition that if you are charging Harbour dues you ought to provide Harbour facilities?'— 'Yes, we do.' 'What do you provide?'—'Well, the Harbour is there. There are moorings there and there is a Harbour supervisor there if he he is required.'

Further questions and answers then established that boatmen provided their own moorings, and that the main function of the Harbour supervisor was to jam cars in on the Harbour car parks, which usually prevented the monks from having vehicular access to their crane. He also collected rents and was not employed on the Harbour in the winter, so that there was a positive absence of facilities for people using the Harbour.

> Mr Elwyn Jones quoted from a letter written by Mr Claye, the former Town clerk, to the Caldey Community's solicitors in September 1957, when he stated that no improvements to the Harbour were contemplated.
>
> Mr Eastlake: 'In my opinion improvements were contemplated.'

'Then do you know why this misleading letter was sent?'—'I cannot answer that.'

Mr Jones suggested that Mr Eastlake had himself taken a rather high-handed attitude when a request was made to him for information by the Community's solicitors. He had replied stating that he had no intention of supplying the information referred to.

Mr Eastlake said that he considered he was not obliged to answer questions on the general administration of the Civic Centre.

Mr Jones: 'The information you gave the Inspector today you could have given us a year ago?' 'I could have done.'

After this came reference to the need for dredging of the Harbour and the 'massive item' of loan charges amounting to £5,000 in the previous six years in respect of demolishing the Victoria Pier. The report then continued:

During further cross-examination, Mr Eastlake said that the Council felt that people earning a good living from the Harbour should not be subsidised by the general ratepayers of Tenby.

Mr Jones: 'What would be the influence on your approach if it were the case that so far as the Caldey Community are concerned they are running a very large deficit each year and cannot make both ends meet?' 'I don't know what to say about that. You do surprise me, that is all I know.'

'If you thought for instance that the Caldey Community were in debt last year to the tune of over £2,000, would that affect your view?' 'No, I am afraid it would not.'

Here, of course, was the crux of much of the problem. Because the monks had considerably increased their business activities, people who knew nothing about business, with its sometimes heavy financial commitments, immediately supposed that they must be making spectacular profits. In fact, although the Caldey Community achieved financial independence and autonomy in 1959, it was not until the early '60's that they were able to show a modest profit. Fr Anthony told the Inspector that although they had not written to the Borough Council on this situation ('I would have been frankly sceptical of the value of writing to Tenby Council.' [Laughter]), he had approached the Deputy Mayor, Mr Ivor Crockford. Mr Crockford was himself a Tenby boatman, but not a member of the 'Pool' of boats running to Caldey, the owners of which would be affected by the proposed new charges.

For some time previous to this the monks had been making limited use of a D.U.K.W., an amphibious craft commonly known as a 'Duck', in the hope that it might help them to overcome some of their problems of insularity in certain weather and tide conditions. In the February of 1960, before the result of the Enquiry became known, the Council suddenly decided to erect bollards across the slipway to the Castle Sands, the beach at which the 'Duck' had been landing instead of using the Harbour. This prevented the monks from using the 'Duck', and correspondence and discussion then had to be entered into which established the legal rights of the monks in the matter. Mainly as a result of this the monks sought a formal lease on the foreshore at Caldey in case their position there could be affected. The Crown Commissioners declined to grant this and said they were already in the process of arranging a lease in favour of the County Council. Further research into Island records then brought to light a rather interesting situation which, in effect, meant that the Crown Commissioners were in no position to grant a lease to anybody because the foreshores on Caldey belonged to the Island anyway. This dated to the grant by Henry I, which had excluded Caldey, together with other lands and hereditaments belonging to the Abbot of St Dogmael's, from all civil jurisdiction in perpetuity.

Subsequently, on the Dissolution of the monasteries, Henry VIII disregarded the grant of Henry I and granted Caldey to John Bradshaw of Presteigne. Apart from demanding all the lead from its buildings, however, Henry VIII, in the grant, signed in his own hand, allowed John Bradshaw to enjoy all the privileges hitherto granted to Caldey by Henry I. This included 'waste' and, according to a judgement of 1858, 'waste ground is desolate and uncultivated.' The Commissioners declared that they were not proceeding with any claim.

One of the barges used for the slipway at Caldey extends slightly beyond the winter low tide mark, and the monks agreed to pay a rental of five shillings a year for this. A very important result of this clarification of the position, however, is that the beaches on Caldey right down to low water mark, are private property and may not be used without permission of the Caldey Community, a fact which, had it been realised at the time, could have saved the Community and Col. Hugo Allen a great deal of trouble back in 1936.

In April 1960, the press were able to report that the Ministry of Agriculture, although there had been no announcement, would be publishing a Draft Order confirming new charges in relation to the use of Tenby Harbour. It was therefore decided to prepare to present a 'memorial' to Parliament on behalf of twenty house-holders of Tenby. This would have had to be presented to both House of Parliament, and would have had the effect of delaying the signing of any Order very considerably. It could also have resulted in the terms of the Order being varied.

The late Desmond Donnelly, at that time Labour M.P. for Pembrokeshire, was brought into the picture, and many letters passed between Government departments and legal gentlemen. Eventually, Tenby Borough Council decided to negotiate. The monks had never questioned their moral obligation to pay for the use of the Harbour. All they had asked for was a fair solution amicably reached. It was agreed that they should pay the Council £300 per year, this figure being based roughly on the amount of produce they were shipping through the Harbour at that time. In the course of discussions it was noted that the Council intended, now that they had demolished the Victoria Pier, to erect some structure to be built into the sea, which could be reached by boats all the time, that the sluice would be improved, and a new crane installed.

The 'memorial' was withdrawn on the understanding that no further steps would be taken to sign the Order. Later, the Order was amended.

In the winter of 1961 the monks discontinued their poultry enterprise and, after a few years, they asked their legal advisers whether they could now expect a reduction in the amount they paid annually to Tenby Council, bearing in mind that the figure had been based partly on the large number of chickens being shipped to the mainland. They also drew attention to a point which seemed to have escaped notice previously, namely that, whereas the members of the 'Pool' were charged for taking visitors to Caldey, no such charge was levied on the other boatmen taking people on trips elsewhere. Their solicitors took counsel's opinion on this point, and they were advised that there was little they could do or for which they could hope. That was in February 1964. Relief, however, was soon to come from an unexpected quarter. The Tenby Council itself.

Fr Anthony had left Caldey in 1962 to become a parish priest, and to Fr Stephen, who had been appointed Procurator in his place, now fell the task of working in harness with Br Thomas.

In 1964, Mr Wynne Samuel was appointed Town Clerk and, in April 1965, he wrote to say that the Council had decided to terminate the agreement forthwith.

Having given notice of the termination of the agreement, the new Town Clerk went on to say:

> I have further to inform you, that the termination of this Agreement will not affect in substance your rights as enumerated in Clause Two of the said Agreement. I am instructed to inform you that the Council is prepared to allow the terms of Clause Two to continue in operation until a new Order comes into operation.
>
> The Council do not intend in any way to disturb your use of the Harbour, and I will be glad if you will let me know that you are prepared to continue your use of of the Harbour in the terms set out in Clause Two.
>
> If you require any further clarification on this matter, I would be pleased to discuss this matter with you or your representatives at my office at a convenient time.
>
> I can, however, assure you that it is not the intention of Tenby Borough Council to disturb relations between your good selves and the Council in any way, except that the Council are now determined to implement their full powers under the above-mentioned Acts in relation to the collection of embarkation fees.

The termination of the agreement was made on very tenuous grounds, and could easily have been contested had anyone wished to do so, but the monks had no desire to. It was unilateral action which suited them very well.

Under the agreement of 1960, the boatmen of the 'Pool' were supposed to present figures, audited by the accountants to the Caldey Community, to the Tenby Council annually. The boatmen had neglected to do this. The accountants, however, could hardly be blamed for not having audited accounts which they had never seen. The Community could be blamed still less.

Fr Stephen accepted the Town Clerk's invitation to discuss

The 'Cottage' Monastery and Church: above, before and below, after
the fire of September 25th, 1940.

The burnt-out church.

The Tenby firemen and volunteers who fought the fire on Caldey.

Taking pigs to the mainland in the 'Crimson Rambler', April 1941.

The wreck of the 'Crimson Rambler' at Eel Point, May 1943.

An amphibious craft on Caldey during the D Day rehearsals off the Pembrokeshire coast.

The burial, without a coffin, of Dom Aelred le Fevre, March 1st, 1942.

Dom Albert Derzelle, Prior of Caldey,
1946 to 1954.

The temporary church as it was in 1949.

The old combine harvester in need of a helping hand, 1954.

Photo: John Topham Ltd.

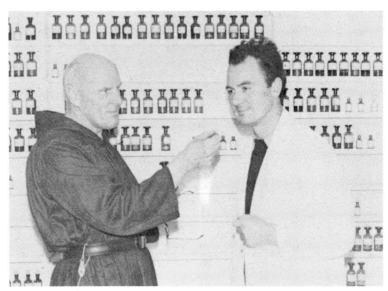

Brother Thomas (left) and Henry Kobus, two of the originators of the
perfume industry, *c.*1955.

Dom James Wicksteed, first Cistercian Abbot of Caldey being
received by Pope John in 1962.

The Community in 1963.

A local wedding, held on the island. *Photo: Squibbs Stud*

Top: The original kitchen range which the Cistercians inherited in 1929.
Centre: The Esse range installed in 1937.
Bottom: The modern electric equipment being used in 1975.

The last picture of Br. Thomas, the first English Professed monk,
taken only days before he died in July, 1966.

Photo: W. P. English

Local ministers and clergy on their way to Caldey for an ecumenical
service in February, 1965.

Photo: Squibbs Studios

The monks at work in the island perfumery.

The herd of Jersey cattle coming from milking at the island farm,
October 1975.

One of the monk's cells, 1975.

Fr. Robert showing the island dairy produce at the West Wales Catering Exhibition, Tenby, 1975.

The landing stage constructed from sunken barges, 1975.

View from the Abbey across the tea gardens and perfume shop to Tenby.

A visitor using the island post box.

Three merry monks in the kitchen. Left to right, Fr. Anselm, Br.
Stanislaus and Fr. Pascal, taken in October 1975.

Making cheese in the modern dairy, 1975.

Above Caldey in the late 19th century, and below approximately the same view in 1975.

the matter, and a misunderstanding immediately arose. It is clear from copies of correspondence kept on Caldey that Fr Stephen was firmly of the opinion that he had gone along merely to listen to the Town Clerk's proposals in order to report them to the Community and their solicitors, and on no account to agree with them without further discussion. The Town Clerk, however, followed up this meeting by writing to the Community's solicitors saying:

> Further to your letter of the 4th May and previous letters referring to the above matter, Father Stephens of Caldey called to see me this morning and, subject to your confirmation, it was agreed that, apart from the discontinuation of collecting embarkation fees, the Community would be allowed to enjoy all the privileges as hitherto.

The letter then went on to enumerate certain conditions, more or less on the lines of the 1960 Agreement, and calling for a payment of £300 before October 1965, together with an intimation of the Council's intention to draw up a new Order to come into effect for the 1966 season. When it was drawn to the attention of the Town Clerk that Fr Stephen denied having entered into any such agreement, he wrote to the Community's solicitors saying:

> I thank you for your letter of the 1st of June, and note the comment made by Fr Stephen. Under the circumstances, I must ask that, in future, all negotiations must take place in writing between your good selves and the Council.

By this time Caldey Island Estates had paid the sum of £50, which they considered covered their right to ply two boats between the Harbour and the Island.

The question of the inequity of the situation had already been taken up previously. Within a year of the Agreement of 1960 being signed, Mr A. L. James, solicitor to the 'Pool' boatmen, and Br Thomas had seen the other signatory, Councillor J. M. Lawrence, the then Mayor:

> And complained that it was manifestly unfair to expect the relevant part of the Agreement dealing with embarkation fees to

be fulfilled so long as there were other boatmen running for reward from Tenby Harbour who were not providing the Council with a similar statement, or even any payment whatsoever for embarkation fees. Councillor Lawrence agreed and said that he would deal with the matter.

The Mayor, however, died suddenly during his year of office and was succeeded by the Deputy Mayor, Councillor Ivor Crockford. The Caldey 'Pool' had never been recognised by the Tenby Borough Council and, in a long letter to the Town Clerk, the Community's solicitor made reference to this point and said:

> We are instructed that at a later date the late Mayor, Councillor Lawrence, agreed with Mr James and Brother Thomas that compliance with the provisions of Clause I should be waived so long as (which was a fact) other boatmen (including the Deputy Mayor, Councillor Ivor Crockford) were running for reward from Tenby Harbour without providing a similar statement or paying any embarkation fee.

The matter, as so often happens in such cases, does not seem to have been pursued at that stage, and nothing was done until the termination of the Agreement by the Borough Council. The Town Clerk then endeavoured to obtain a temporary agreement which would bring in as much revenue as previously and, in a letter to the Community's solicitors, referred to 'very wide powers' which the Council had in the control of the Harbour, suggesting that a sum of £150 was due for six months of the unexpired part of the year of the Agreement which, of course, had now been terminated.

The Community's solicitors argued that the Council, having repudiated the Agreement, were now put back upon their statutory rights and this would have meant collecting all money themselves at the time of shipment. There would not have been sufficient money collected to cover the cost of collecting it, which would not have been particularly good business, even by municipal standards. Caldey had already paid £50, and figures of shipments showed that charges due would have fallen far short of the £150 being demanded. It should also be noted that the solicitors had already offered, on behalf of the Community, either to render an annual statement or pay an annual sum based on an average of the previous three years.

In the very long letter already referred to, the solicitors spelled out the position quite clearly and fairly, and concluded by saying:

> Whilst we appreciate the difficulties facing the Council over the administration of the Harbour, we would emphasise that our clients' desire to be reasonable must not be rebuffed by any proposal which is patently inequitable.

The date of the letter was July 21st, 1965. On July 24th, the Town Clerk replied saying:

> I acknowledge receipt of your letter of the 21st July. It would appear that your clients do not appreciate the facilities which Tenby Borough Council have extended to them in the past.
>
> It would further appear that there is no common basis for agreement, and consequently there can be little purpose in my replying in detail to the points you raise in your letter.
>
> I am instructed by H.W. The Mayor [*Mr Ivor Crockford*] to inform you that the Council will, on Tuesday, 27th July, consider:
>
> 1. The withdrawal of all discretionary rights and privileges granted to your clients.
>
> 2. The immediate implementation of strict rules and statutory obligations as between your Clients and my Council.

The solicitors replied:

> We have your letter of the 24th instant. It is a little difficult for our clients to appreciate the facilities to which you refer, without knowing exactly what they are. If you would care to specify them in detail we will, of course, get into touch with our clients.
>
> We note that, in the last paragraph of your letter, you refer to 'all discretionary rights and privileges granted'. It would certainly assist us if you could let us know exactly what is meant by this expression.

The Town Clerk's reply to this letter was dated July 29th, 1965. The same day saw the erection of a barrier on the Harbour which prevented the monks having access by vehicle between their crane and their storehouse. This right was explicit in the Agreement of 1931 relating to the crane and, thanks to the goodwill of some of the Councillors, the situation was quickly rectified and the Harbour Superintendent given instructions to lift the barrier whenever required to do so by employees of the Caldey Community.

In his letter of July 29th the Town Clerk referred to a decision reached by the Harbour and Pier Committee, of which the Mayor was chairman, and having reiterated the previous demands and conditions, including £300 per year for the use of the Harbour, went on to say:

> In the alternative, if your clients will not agree to the said payment, the Council will enforce all the statutory regulations connected with the Harbour and Pier, and the cancellation of all the discretionary rights and privileges hitherto granted to your clients. The alternative would come into operation on the 1st day of September 1965, and the effect would be:
>
> (a) The regulation charges will be made per boat per entry to the Harbour.
>
> (b) The introduction of a time-table to regulate the use of the Pier by your clients.
>
> (c) The shipment, transhipment or unshipment of goods to be limited to three days per week, namely Monday, Wednesday and Friday and at such times to be determined by the Harbour Master.
>
> (d) The payment of embarkation fees by all persons resident or working or employed at Caldey Island, or visiting Caldey for any purpose whatsoever.
>
> (e) Under the terms of the Harbour (Amendment) Order, 1960, it shall be a condition that no coal, goods, vegetables, fruit, etc., be accepted without the payment of the appropriate charge and the production of a Weight ticket from a public Weighbridge in respect of each and every item specified in the Order. [*There is no public Weighbridge in Tenby*].
>
> (f) In future your clients shall not be allowed to use the Harbour or the Pier for any purpose whatever without the Statutory and Regulation payment being made. These will include charges for use of the Pier by lorries, parking of cars, etc.
>
> (g) The Regulation charges will be applied for all mooring space west of the the Pier.
>
> (h) That your Clients be asked to remove the crane (which is solely used by them) from Tenby Pier, and that that part of the Pier be restored to its original state.

(i) That the right to use Castle Sands for amphibious craft be terminated forthwith.

(j) The strict enforcement of the regulation which applies to Licences granted. I must point out that the 'Isle of Caldey' and the 'Menevia' are licensed to carry passengers only. The licence does not permit the carriage of goods, etc., by these boats.

The effect of the alternative will be to impose on your clients precisely the same regulations as would apply to any other user of the Harbour under similar circumstances.

I am further instructed to inform you that the above alternative offers are final.

Several points now arose. It involved the monks' contract with the Postmaster General to carry Her Majesty's Mails. There was also an arrangement with the Ministry of Transport to carry Her Majesty's Coastguards on their tours of duty. Furthermore, the only other vessel regularly using the Harbour during the winter months was the R.A.F. Air Sea Rescue Launch, so that, according to the Town Clerk's letter, they would also seem to be affected by any restrictions imposed on the monks.

There had previously been a weighbridge near the Pier, but this had been removed and the office let out as an ice-cream kiosk. If the threatened action had been implemented, the onus of providing a weighbridge would have fallen upon the Council as the Harbour Authority.

Unknown to the people of Tenby, the Caldey Community at that time were under some pressure from influential people within their Order to close the Island to day-visitors and to keep it for one of its original purposes, namely the holding of religious retreats and conferences without disturbance. There were members of the Community who were of the same opinion, and it was known that Rome would have looked favourably upon such a move. The Abbot, however, felt keenly that this would have a serious effect on the livelihood of a number of Tenby boatmen and detract, to some extent at least, from Tenby as a seaside resort. There was now so much goodwill amongst the Tenby people towards the monks that such a step would only have been taken as a last resort. It would, of course, have had an effect on the monks' income, but the perfume industry was by this time well-established and, given freedom from the need to cater for such a huge influx of visitors, the monks could have expanded this new enterprise which, as it has been seen, was so suitable to the Island economy. It would also have meant using Saundersfoot Harbour, which would have increased the monks' difficulties and costs, but it would have been possible.

All the correspondence between the monks and their solicitors shows quite clearly that they had at all times been most anxious to act within the law and to conform with all proper regulations controlling the use of the Harbour and Pier. In replying to the Town Clerk's letter, the Community's solicitors asked for enlightenment on many points concerning the wide powers and facilities referred to, together with evidence that the crane was used solely by the monks. The letter concluded:

> Please let us have specific answers on the above queries as soon as possible. At the moment, our Clients take a very serious view of your letter. They would regret if any attempt to compel their agreement to the payment of sums in excess of those which the Council is authorised to levy should force them to contemplate the adoption of any measure which might react upon the amenities offered by Tenby to visitors or upon the welfare of its boatmen. Our Clients would regard it as no less a matter for regret if they were compelled to have recourse to the appropriate Government Authority for the settlement of a matter which should and, given goodwill, could be settled amicably.

In the course of his reply, dated August 18th, the Town Clerk said:

> Referring to paragraphs 1-5 in your letter of the 4th August, I regret that I do not consider it to be my duty, after all our correspondence, to prove my Council's Authority and powers to implement all the conditions noted in my letter to you dated the 29th July under paragraph 2. Should their implementation become necessary, and you consider that any one, or all, rest outside the jurisdiction of my Council, I am sure you will advise your Clients as to their remedies.
>
> I regret that your Clients are disturbed by the tone of my letter of the 29th July. With very great respect, may I add that I have often had cause to be exasperated by some of the comments and arguments which have appeared in your letters, and by what would appear to

be your constant attempts to belittle the contribution made and the facilities offered by my Council in the past.

In the event, the recommendations of the Harbour and Pier Committee were not confirmed by the Council and an attempt was made to continue negotiations. By this time, however, the position had become so intolerable that the monks had again enlisted the aid of their M.P., Desmond Donnelly, and raised the matter with the Ministry of Agriculture, whilst the affair at local level dragged along its weary and seemingly interminable way.

On January 31st, 1966, a meeting took place in the Council Offices between the Mayor, Deputy Mayor, the Town Clerk, Fr Stephen and Br Thomas. [*The Deputy Mayor at this time was the late Mr Colwyn Williams, who had been Mayor in 1963. He was one of those who had intervened in the nonsense of the barrier which had been erected at the harbour the previous summer. He was a Group Secretary with the National Farmers' Union and, in that capacity, had been a great help to the Community in the Union's support of them at the Public Enquiry in 1959.*] The only positive outcome subsequently, however, seems to have been the threat of legal action by the Town Clerk and/or the Borough Council against the Community's solicitors.

Certain proposals were discussed at this meeting, without agreement being reached, but, as a gesture of goodwill, and not in any way admitting liability for the Council's claim, the Caldey representatives agreed to pay the sum of £125 purported to be outstanding under the former agreement and covering the period October 1964 to April 1965.

At the conclusion of the meeting the Caldey representatives were told that the various proposals discussed would be considered at a meeting of the Council, and the monks informed at the earliest possible moment of the Council's proposals.

No communication was received, but a month later the attention of the Community was drawn to a report in *The Tenby Observer* to the effect that , after considering the matter in private, the Council had entered into a new agreement with the Caldey Community. The monks' solicitors thought it advisable to ask for an explanation, and wrote to the Town Clerk accordingly on March 15th:

We learn from our clients that a meeting took place on 31st January last between them and yourself, the Mayor and Deputy Mayor, that at this meeting certain proposals were discussed with a view to exploring the possibility of an amicable settlement dealing with (a) the period from October 1964 to April 1965 and (b) the period thereafter, and that, no definite agreement having been reached, you would be writing to our clients with the Council's proposals.

Our clients are still awaiting this promised letter, which they would like to have as soon as you are able to write it.

In the meantime, there has been drawn to our clients' notice, a statement in the local Press dated 25th February, which they are wholly at a loss to understand.

We enclose a copy of this statement and would draw your particular attention to the words that following upon the above meeting 'the matter was considered in private' and 'A new agreement with Caldey Estate for payment of dues has been entered into by the Town Council'!

The report, as you will see, then goes on to refer to certain terms of the so-called agreement.

This statement that an agreement has been reached is, of course, wholly inaccurate. Further, the inference to be drawn from the reference to the consideration of the matter in private, is that the Press could only have obtained their information from you, unless there has been an unwarranted leakage.

You will agree that our clients are entitled to a repudiation by you of what is stated in the Press report, together with some explanation of the circumstances in which that statement came to be published.

We shall be glad to hear from you at your early convenience.

The letter from the Town Clerk of March 16th went as follows:

I thank you for your letter of the 15th March and confirm that a meeting took place between the representatives of Caldey Island Estate and representatives of the Council on the 31st January.

The terms which have been discussed by the Council are being sent to Caldey Island Estate this day, a copy of which is enclosed for your information.

I note your reference to the press report. I am in no way responsible for what appears in the press and I resent your accusation that the information could only have been received from me. I require an apology for this statement.

If your clients feel aggrieved by the press report, that is a matter for them to remedy.

There then ensued a series of somewhat acrimonious letters in which the solicitors denied having made the accusations which the Town Clerk claimed they had made, whilst the Town Clerk threatened to report the matter to his union. Following this dire threat, it was next reported in the local paper that the Mayor and members of the Council, along with the Town Clerk, were to seek an apology.

It culminated during the following month in a letter from the Town Clerk, dated April 7th:

> I acknowledge receipt of your letter of 31st March and note that you have no intention of withdrawing your offending remarks made in your letter dated 15th March, or to tender an apology. Accordingly I am reporting the matter again to the Council. [*Desperate measures indeed—R.H.*]

History thereafter remains mercifully silent on the subject.

The press report, of course, was quite accurate except that agreement had not been reached. The terms were all accurate, however, and the Community had readily agreed to all of them except the one in which they would be required to pay £350 a year for the use of the Harbour and Pier. The Town Clerk's letter of March 16th actually said, '£350 for three years', and this was also the wording of the newspaper report, but Fr Stephen drew attention to this, and the Town Clerk agreed that what he had really meant was '£350 a year for three years'. And this figure was completely unacceptable to the Community.

The following month Fr Stephen and Br Thomas attended a meeting of the Council's General Purposes Committee to discuss the position further, but no progress was made.

All this, of course, also affected those Tenby boatmen who were in the 'Pool' of boats running to Caldey. One of them, Mr Noel Crockford, who had many years' association with the monks, and was a brother of the Mayor (who was not in the 'Pool'!), asked the 'Pool's' solicitors to raise the issue. In his reply, the Town Clerk wrote, 'The Council are not concerned with any Association that may exist.'

Meanwhile Desmond Donnelly was already busy and contemplating raising the matter in the House. On June 8th, James Hoy, Parliamentary Secretary to the Minister of Agriculture, wrote to to him saying:

> The charges which are legally payable by the monks are those listed in the schedule to the Tenby Harbour (Amendment) Order 1960, two copies of which I enclose. The monks' total legal liability under the Order will accordingly be determined by the turnover in goods and passengers conveyed.

On June 14th the Borough Council's General Purposes Committee decided to elect a new standing Harbour Committee, in place of the old Harbour Sub-Committe and this would report direct to the Council. Although there was some discussion on the advisability of someone with a particular interest in the Harbour being appointed to the Chair, the Mayor was eventually, on a vote, elected Chairman.

On June 17th Fr Stephen received by registered post a letter from the Town Clerk stating that the terms outlined in his letter of March 16th, and in accordance with the Tenby Harbour Act 1838 and Tenby Harbour (Amendment) Order 1960, were to come into force immediately. This could not, of course, have been strictly accurate because the letter, dated June 15th, went on to say:

> The use of Tenby Harbour by the Caldey Island Estate, shall henceforth be subject to the conditions of management as required by the Harbourmaster. The Payment of all dues, tolls, etc., shall be made to the Harbourmaster in accordance with the above-mentioned Act and Order, the time of the shipment or transhipment of goods, etc. The other provisions contained in the said Act and Order will also be applied to persons embarking from Tenby Harbour.

This was, in fact, somewhat at variance with the letter of March 16th which had asked for an annual payment (when clarified) of £350 a year.

Fr Stephen sent the letter to the Community's solicitors and, in the course of his covering letter, said:

I wonder if you would also be good enough to draft a reply to Mr
Samuel's letter, stating that we are willing to co-operate with the
Harbour Master, but would like him to be more explicit about the
payment of Dues: do the Council wish us to pay for each shipment
as and when it is unshipped or shipped in Tenby Harbour? It is
important to know this in order to avoid the Harbour Master
preventing us from moving cargo on or off the pier. I shall also
warn the Community that, contrary to their vow of Poverty, they
will now be required by lesser authority to carry pocket money.

At this juncture a great peace seemed to descend upon the
proceedings with news that George Thomas, the Secretary of
State for Wales, through Desmond Donnelly's good offices,
had accepted an invitation to visit Caldey and have lunch
there, when he would be accompanied by the Mayor (like Mr
Thomas and Mr Donnelly, a member of the Labour Party) and
the Town Clerk (like Mr George Thomas, a Nonconformist lay
preacher).

When the visit eventually took place in September, the
Secretary of State undertook to intervene personally if there
should be any further dispute about the Harbour. Before the
visit took place, however, Br Thomas, as recorded earlier, died
with tragic suddenness, on his way to the boat. The spontaneous
reaction of the Borough Council, and the widespread sympathy
of the vast majority of people on the mainland, were the real
indication of the regard and affection which they had, not only
for this remarkable monk, but for the Community with which
he had for so long been synonymous.

At the Harbour, dues were collected daily, and it was seen
that the monks' assessment of what they should have been
paying had been accurate, and the civic authorities were able to
see the mistake they had made in not accepting what had been
a very fair offer.

Talk of the Council providing their own crane, however,
once having started, then continued. At their December
meeting Clr. M. B. Eastlake, who had by now retired from his
post of Borough Accountant and been elected a member, had
apparently forgotten the case he had promoted on the subject
seven years earlier at the 1959 Public Enquiry, and observed:
'The crane seems to be for Caldey and why should we install a
crane for Caldey? I'm damned if I know.'

The much-discussed civic crane eventually became a reality in the summer of 1967, and by this time the real issues had been forgotten and there were people who genuinely believed that they were helping the monks by installing it. Its acquisition was not without its problems, chief amongst them being that whenever a suitable machine was located, by the time the sub-committee deputed to inspect it had been able to report back and get a decision, the machine would have been sold to someone else, and then the procedure had to start all over again. The crane eventually acquired cost £2,000 and had an insured life of five years. It was not long before the Council were asking the monks if their employees could help by operating the crane on a part-time basis. And it was not a very good crane, either. Long before it had reached the end of its insured life the idea was being mooted that it would be more satisfactory for the monks to provide their own crane, and the *status quo* was eventually resumed.

The monks had given their old crane to the Council in 1967 and the same happy relationship still existed. But the Harbour was not without its problems in other spheres. Much of the trouble arose because of differences between boatmen who either were or were not in the 'Pool' running to Caldey. Whatever these differences may have been, it has to be remembered that the existence of the 'Pool' was the only simple and practical method at the monks' disposal to limit the maximum number of visitors to the Island in any one day.

In 1969 new Harbour charges were introduced and the Tenby Harbour Users' Association was formed in order to resist them and to protect the Users' interests. The 'Pool' boat owners were prominent members, and Fr Stephen was appointed the Association's Secretary.

The Council, of course, had to submit their proposals to the Minister of Agriculture. The Harbour Users objected and, in 1970, another Public Enquiry was held. The Council probably did nothing to help their case, if they had one, by implementing the charges before the Enquiry was held, and Desmond Donnelly reported the matter to the Ombudsman.

Understandably, this created something of a sensation, and the matter was not without its amusing sidelights. By this time Mr Donnelly, although continuing as M.P. for Pembrokeshire, had left the Labour Party and formed his own, short-lived, Democratic Party. The Chairman of the Harbour Committee, Mr Ivor Crockford, had joined it and was now somewhat embarrassed by his Leader's latest action. The Town Clerk had meanwhile been adopted as the Welsh Nationalist candidate for the forthcoming Parliamentary election and condemned this action on the part of his political opponent as being 'irresponsible'. All of which internecine skullduggery, of course, had little enough to do with the monks who suffered nevertheless as the result.

The Enquiry was held in September 1970, and the case for the Council was put by the Town Clerk. The only witness he called was the Borough Treasurer. The proceedings were fully reported and no useful purpose would be served in writing of them here. The Inspector, Col. Trevor Kelway, in his report to the Minister, had:

> no hesitation in recommending that the Minister should decide that the Objections of the Tenby Harbour Users' Association should be UPHELD, and that the increased Harbour dues and charges imposed by the Tenby Harbour Authority as from the 1st April, 1970, should NOT be approved.

The Inspector also recommended, and the Minister accepted, that the Borough Council should meet all the costs of the Enquiry.

With the reorganisation of Local Government, control of Tenby Harbour became the responsibility of the new South Pembrokeshire District Council.

Although the account of this protracted interlude in the monks' affairs has resulted in a long chapter, it could well have been considerably longer. Much has been omitted in an endeavour to avoid becoming too tedious, but the effort has been made to give, overall, a fair picture.

One thing is certain: throughout lengthy research into a vast number of letters, Council minutes, agreements and reports, there has never been the slightest indication of anything other than a sincere desire on the part of the monks to behave in an honourable and reasonable way. It has also been abundantly clear that all they desired, and strove hard to achieve, was a fair arrangement amicably reached. Readers must decide for themselves whether this fair arrangement might have been possible without the very great expense and trouble to which they must have been subjected. It has unfortunately been necessary to write of these matters at some length because they involved two Public Enquiries, which received national news coverage, and it was not possible to give an idea of what was involved without going into some considerable detail.

15
FINANCIAL STABILITY AT LAST

'For which of you, intending to build a tower, sitteth not down first, and counteth the cost, whether he have sufficient to finish it?':
Luke 14:28

During the events related in the preceding chapter, life on Caldey went on in much the same way as it had always done, just as the monastic life had been pursued there during the troubles of the first decade of the Community's existence. Most of the Community would have known little, if anything, of the problems being grappled with by those who had to deal with the outside world.

One great achievement was to have demonstrated that they could be financially self-supporting. Whilst many monastic Communities have been able to do this, the costs on an island, depending on commerce and trade with the mainland, were bound to be higher, and the difficulty that much greater. Caldey, because of this insularity, is in many ways unique, and to have made a financial success of an island can be nothing but cause for admiration. And all the time, as the Community struggled on, they became more and more closely identified with their mainland neighbours in Tenby.

Reference has already been made to the great contribution made by Br Thomas towards this end, and the warmth of the feeling towards the Community when he died in July 1966, at a time when the casual observer could have been forgiven for thinking there was antagonism, was manifestly evident in the reaction to the news at his sudden passing.

Led by the Mayor in his own boat, a gay flag-bedecked little fleet of pleasure craft carried a representative gathering across to Caldey for the funeral, for which the normal privacy of a monk's burial was not observed. As 'Brother' would have wished, it was a joyful occasion and Fr Vince, Catholic priest of Tenby at that time and a close friend, said in his farewell tribute, 'If he thought I was to stand here uttering pious platitudes he would turn in his grave.' Then, urging that there should be no lament, and having said that Br Thomas would not put up with the 'petty frustrations of purgatory', he said:

> Most surely by now he has talked and stormed his way into Heaven, there besieging—not beseeching—the Almighty to fill the gaps left by his death in our hearts and in our midsts.
> In our hearts because he was a true friend, a guide, an advisor, a giver of hope, a great enlivener.
> In our midst because in the Community, on the Island, in Tenby, on the Harbour, in the Parish, in the Church, among the Churches, he was a great planner and a builder.

'Brother' was fifty-seven when he died of a heart attack, and those who knew of his apparently rude good health and imagined him living to a ripe old age, found it difficult to understand. Those better acquainted with the position, however, knew that he had strained his heart some years previously when struggling to save the monks' boat, the 'Lollipop'. The boat had been left at her moorings overnight because there would be no water in Tenby harbour in the morning when she would be needed, and rough weather had blown up. He was never the same again. It is all part of the high price which the islander has to pay.

The 'Lollipop', given to the monks by Mr. Walter Roch, who had also given them their boat back in 1936, became very well-known during the 1950s when Caldey was being widely featured in magazines and on television. They took delivery of her in 1951 and when she was wrecked, in a summer storm ten years later, it was an event which featured prominently in the news. A few days later a young man turned up in the post office on Caldey asking if he could see a monk. No, he didn't know which monk. Just any monk. Well, it was about money and a boat. So Fr. Anthony, the Procurator, was sent for and, when he arrived, the young man said, 'I'm from Barry Island fun-fair. My father was very upset to hear about you losing your boat so he organised a collection and he's sent me down with the money to help you to buy a new one.' And he gave Fr. Anthony a bag which contained one hundred pounds.

The boy was young John Collins, who had just passed his driving test and was being entrusted by his father to go on a man's errand for the first time. His father, John Collins senior, was the son of Patrick Collins, who used to take his showman's outfit every year to the famous Mop at Stratford and became a close friend of the Abbot's father who was a Shakespearian actor there.

Boats, of course, have always been an integral feature of the monks' life on Caldey. Unlike those who sought to make a living on the other Pembrokeshire islands, the monks were fortunate in having the use of larger boats because they had the benefit of the safer anchorage at Tenby Harbour, whilst those on the other islands were more restricted in the size of boats it was possible to keep. This is why the monks' boats have always been kept at Tenby, apart from during war-time when restrictions resulted in the closing of the Harbour to private craft and necessitated the keeping of the boat at Caldey. Even so, they have had other losses over the years. They lost the 'Teresina' in the early days, then the 'Caldey Abbey', and then the 'Crimson Rambler' before the 'Lollipop'.

The other achievement has been to succeed, albeit after many vicissitudes, in establishing an English-speaking foundation. In spite of this, and a degree of financial independence, the pursuit of monastic aims has not been easy. Whereas, by 1960, the numbers had reached forty, that number was to decline to twenty. With the scale of commercial activity necessary to make the Island pay, this led in turn to the necessity to employ more labour, which is something which must be of concern to the monks because, apart from the expense, there is always the danger of a situation developing in which they find themselves in the position of their feudal predecessors, when Lords of the Manor had serfs to work for them, and when monks were employers on some scale. It is perhaps one reason why the present Community do not much care for the title of Lord of the Manor to which the Abbot of Caldey can lay claim. And it must remain as one of their aims to achieve that ideal situation in which they do all the manual work themselves. Although that aim may well be an ideal rather than a possibility, the less far they have to depart from it, the happier they must be. As Van Zeller has written:

> If the activities on which Benedictines are engaged, today or at any other time, are more concerned to serve secular rather than

religious ends, they will eventually kill the idea from which they sprang. That system which turns a Benedictine monk into a commercial enterprise, or which views its Benedictine name in a political interest, or which views its Benedictine subjects as operatives rather than as souls, is doomed. Economically and socially it may not fail—indeed it may prosper—but so far as its Benedictine character goes it cannot last.

It will perhaps come as a surprise to some people, as it apparently did to the Borough Accountant at the 1960 Public Enquiry, that up to the early 1960's the monks were still losing money. It is to be hoped that sufficient has been written in these pages for it to be possible more readily to understand some of the problems involved and to accept that, contrary to popular belief, the monks are not making very much money. The maintenance of two boats, with three men to be paid all the year round, is one item which does not have to be met by the business or monastery on the mainland, and this takes an appreciable slice out of what might otherwise be profit. Then again, property maintenance is a costly item anywhere, and much work has had to be done on the Abbey and other buildings of recent years. And much work, if there are not enough monks to do the work themselves, means much expense.

To make it a little more attractive and comfortable for the small number of employees on the Island, a club has been provided for them. Guests on the Island, for certain very good reasons, are asked not to make use of this. Because the club is licensed, alcoholic beverages may be seen from time to time being shipped across from Tenby Harbour, which gives rise to the idea amongst those who wish to believe it that 'the monks are no better than anybody else and there they are laying in booze again'. Likewise, they are reckoned to be 'no better than anybody else' if a monk should be seen walking along the beach talking to a nun whilst waiting for the boat.

It is, of course, an important part of the monks' purpose to provide a spiritual retreat for those in need of it, not only nuns and monks and priests, but many of those for whom society has no time. In all these guests, the monks see Christ and treat them accordingly—'Inasmuch as ye have done unto one of the least of these my brethren ye have done it unto me.' More than a thousand such people are welcomed to Caldey each year and go back amongst their fellow men and women who may also, because of their influence, benefit from this spiritual refreshment that has been found amidst Caldey's peace.

Occasionally, of course, there is the odd one whose only intention is to take advantage of kindness, but, as one monk said, 'I would rather see our hospitality being abused by twenty such types than to think we had become so worldly-wise and cautious as to risk turning our backs on just one who is in need.' And when the odd one arrives to take advantage and is recognised accordingly, it is usually sufficient to mention quietly that most guests like to do a little job towards helping the work of the Community, and Br So-and-So is loading ten tons of potatoes tomorrow and would appreciate a little help. One more passenger for the boat back to the mainland in the morning is a near certainty.

In addition to whatever good has come through the influence of those who have been spiritually refreshed on Caldey, some of the members of the Community have themselves gone out into the world with their good works. If monks are not allowed the human failing of a little occasional pride, they will no doubt be forgiven for at least feeling real pleasure that one of their members, John Gran, became Bishop of Oslo, subsequently to become Head of the Church in Norway. It was the first time for a monk of Caldey to be elected Bishop since St Samson had become Bishop of Dol in the 6th century. Bishop Gran was one of the first four novices after the war who were sent to Chimay and later recalled. Another of them was Dom James Wicksteed, who became Abbot of Caldey in 1959. Although Bishop Gran's appointment in 1963 gave the Community considerable pleasure, it left behind a nice example of the balance between the spiritual and the temporal. 'We have missed him terribly,' said Fr Thaddeus. 'He was a first-class mechanic.'

Another practical difficulty, and one involving considerable expense, was the provision of an adequate supply of water to improve on the meagre flow provided by the one small spring. As livestock increased and a new dairy enterprise was envisaged, and as the day-visitors increased in numbers, so did the water shortage become more acute. During one particularly dry summer, there was a period when the monks had to bath and shave in the sea. In 1961 a firm of civil engineers carried out a survey. It was estimated that, on a catchment area the size of Caldey, something like 450,000,000 gallons of water must fall annually, yet only about 1,500,000 gallons were being used. A budget was drawn up, and for several years money was put on one side to make possible greater utilisation of the water available.

Initially there had been a problem because the only drilling rig in the area weighed eight tons, whilst the Island crane could lift only two tons. Eventually, a smaller rig was found, and drilling was carried out in the autumn of 1974, a local water-diviner, Mr Sidney Thomas, Penally, having pinpointed where he believed the water was. The cost of drilling was £350 per day, and enough money had been set aside to pay for seven days' drilling. That was all the monks could afford although, in the event, it had to go on longer. In that time drilling was carried out in four places and water was found in two of them. It was decided to keep one in reserve and make use of the better one, near lovely Sandtop Bay, where water was found at a hundred and twenty feet, and to pump it by electric motor to a thousand-gallon tank above the farmyard and to storage tanks near the lighthouse, from which it would be fed by gravity to the whole Island.

It is in this question of budgeting that the members of the Community find another example of how carefully they must balance one need against another. Times come when something is needed outside the budget, and then the decision has to be taken as to whether whatever it is must wait to be included in some future budget, or whether the money, being available, may justifiably be spent there and then. Unlike any other business, however, if this course is followed, it is others who will suffer, because all the profits the monks make is given to charity.

To this end the Island was transferred to the Trustees of Caldey, the Abbot and three other monks, in 1971, and established as a charity on terms acceptable to the Inland Revenue. Prior to this the situation had been somewhat anomalous. Usually, when autonomy is granted, the Community take over but, in the case of Caldey, because it had been purchased at the direct request of Rome, ownership remained with the Order at Citeaux.

Again, contrary to a belief held in many quarters, the money does not go 'to swell the coffers of Rome'. Nor does it go exclusively to Catholic charities. Far from it. It goes mainly to 'the little old lady down the road', and to those who have 'slipped through the net of Social Security'. There are surprisingly many of them.

This being so, it is tempting for those who are given to laying down the law about what other people should do, and how they should live, to assert that, of course, the monks ought to concentrate on making even more money. Their vocations would then be more worthwhile, and they would be fulfilling a more useful purpose in life because they would be able to give more to charity.

This may well be so, but they would hardly then be truly monks.

16
DAYS OF CHANGE

'Old things are passed away; behold all things are become new':
2 Corinthians 5:17

Most of us know surprisingly little of other people's work and life and the problems with which they have to contend, and, all too often perhaps, have little interest in them. It is only when the spotlight of public attention is focused on them, not infrequently because of what has become known as industrial action, that the problems are thought about by those not immediately concerned with them. And then, as often as not, they become the concern of the rest of the community because of the inconvenience and hardship they cause. Where people have a grievance and are not in a position to inconvenience others, they usually have to do something a little different in order to attract attention, such as chaining themselves to railings or, in more extreme cases, pouring petrol over themselves and striking a match.

Although monks are frequently accused of having opted out, as though this were some serious offence against society, they do not normally have cause to draw attention to their way of life, and there is therefore no great measure of understanding for what they are trying to do or the way in which they try to do it. It would be wrong, however, to assume that time, for the monks, has stood still completely. There have been changes in some of their ideas and methods, but there are also other fundamental beliefs to which they cling and which nothing on earth could shake.

They still begin their day at quarter past three in the morning, because they know that it is in the mysterious tranquillity of the early hours that the mind is most fresh and receptive to that 'still small voice'. They still devote seven hours of the day to prayer and contemplation, because that is their vocation. They still work hard physically, because that is necessary in order to live.

Besides the physical work, however, there is the more

sophisticated approach towards all business ventures which can make it so much more difficult to follow the monastic calling. To find the right balance must sometimes be very difficult. The tendency is for all businesses to expand, to increase turnover, and to follow certain rules and patterns which seem to be necessary for survival itself. The business consultant would possibly advise that the difficult and not highly remunerative farming business should be abandoned in favour of a greater concentration of effort on the perfume industry, which is so much more suitable to the Island economy. But to do that would be to be unmindful of the fact that the Cistercian is basically an agricultural monk. This being so, there are those who would tell the monks how they ought to manage their farming affairs, just as there are those who will criticise farmers for removing hedgerows and adopting methods of factory farming. The same people are quite content to buy the cheapest possible eggs or chickens from the supermarket or, if they are vegetarians, look for the cheapest lettuce that may have been produced by an under-recouped grower. The monks, too, had their critics when they tried to make money from poultry by using the more modern methods of husbandry.

In any case, if business considerations were all that mattered, a good argument could be put forward for the development of Caldey as a holiday island. With seven sandy beaches and enough land to accommodate who-knows-how-many thousands of caravans, Caldey could do for itself what the National Park and so-called planning have done for the mainland. The prospects are endless, but they are also unspeakable.

In the allocation of their time between prayer and work, the monks' day remains much as it has always done, but, in the carrying out of that work, advantage has been taken of modern equipment and improved techniques. For example, the old-fashioned kitchen range was replaced by a solid-fuel cooker which, in turn, gave way to electric cookers when the mains electricity became available. And this meant being able to cut out the humping of large quantities of coal annually. Use has also been made of modern machinery and equipment in the farming operations, and in many other spheres.

Nowadays there is even a colour television set. But it is watched only on a Sunday afternoon. A video cassette recorder is used to record selected programmes during the week and these are the programmes which the Community see. The mid-day meal is still eaten in silence whilst one of the Community reads aloud but, on Sundays and certain Holy Days and Feast Days, the reading is replaced by classical music played on a stereo record player.

One of the problems which must always occupy the minds of those committed to a life of monasticism is the need to see when change is preferable to continuance in any particular way purely because the Rule lays that way down, especially when it is remembered that, in part, the Rule was written to serve the needs of that particular time, just as Moses laid down his Ten Commandments to serve the needs of the tribes of Israel wandering in the desert. As typical as anything in this respect is the question of clothing.

Originally the monk's habit was adopted because it answered the need for cheapness and simplicity. When wool became dearer, man-made fibre took its place. Even the cheapest habit, however, was destined to become an expensive badge of poverty, with the realisation that in the latter half of the twentieth century there could hardly be anything cheaper than a jumper and jeans or an old-fashioned boiler suit or workman's overalls. To see monks thus attired may destroy the image which so many people have of them, but if that image has, as often as not, been derived from a lack of understanding, it may be no bad thing.

The pure wool tunic, whilst still being retained for church wear for the sake of undistracting uniformity, needed to be dispensed with for ordinary wear, not only because it had become too expensive, but because it was no longer suitable for work in the changed conditions and with the changing require-ments posed by working with modern machinery. On grounds of safety the original habit was eminently unsuitable. Nor is it easy to see what could any longer be achieved spiritually by the monks following that part of the Rule which bids them sleep in the clothes in which they have been working all day, especially if the work has involved cleaning out the pigs. There are bound to be more hygienic ways to Heaven, and less inhibiting prospects for potential recruits. Even John Wesley, the founder of Methodism, advised on the question of neatness of apparel, which he saw as a duty rather than a sin, that 'cleanliness is next to Godliness.'

There has been a considerable measure of rationalisation in the monks' way of life during recent years, and nowadays, therefore, when they retire for the night, they sleep, according to their own choice, either in pyjamas or in singlet and shorts.

On the question of faults, too, there has been evidence of new thinking. All property is communal. At one time it was considered proper that when a Brother, through carelessness or stupidity, had broken a dish or spade or whatever else, he should kneel before his fellows and, holding up whatever he had broken, show himself to be truly contrite. At a time when many monks were of noble birth such a humiliating act may have been no bad thing. But when the time had been reached that the rest of the Community started to pull funny faces at the offending Brother, the ritual had clearly outlived any usefulness it may once have had. Nowadays, therefore, it is considered to be sufficient for the Abbot, in Chapter, to give a short talk and possibly make some small reference to any particular point which he considers to be worth mentioning. For example, rumour has it that when the water-drilling operations, already referred to, were about to commence, the Abbot said to the Community, 'I suppose it would be asking too much of anybody not to see how the work is going, but perhaps it would be better if if you didn't make any suggestions as to how they should do it.'

On the question of silence, too, there has been the same measure of rationalisation and the Community do not follow as strict a Rule in this respect as formerly. Even so, the monastery remains essentially a quiet place, and there is no talking merely for the sake of talking. Certainly there is no small talk or aimless chatter. Monks go about their business with purposefulness, and it would be highly unlikely to come across a group of monks engaged in conversation. Not only is there no gossip, but there is a distinct lack of communication, and this is a point which has already been discussed in more detail. Nor is there idle curiosity. If there is someone staying with the monks, those who do not know who he is will be quite happy that someone of their Community has invited him for a sufficiently good reason, and he will be welcomed by all. Certainly they will not go round speculating amongst themselves as to what the guest's troubles may be, if in fact he is there because he has troubles. If he has, and wishes to talk about them, that is a different matter. Likewise, if a Brother has to go away for any reason, it is unlikely that many of the others will know what that reason is. They may notice that his choir stall is empty, or that he is not in his accustomed place in refectory. If they give this a passing thought that is as far as it goes.

Reference has already been made to those who find their way to Caldey in search of rest, and spiritual help and retreat. More than a thousand people go to Caldey every year in this way. Attached to the monastery, the Abbatial quarters, built by Aelred Carlyle, serve as a guest-house for a small number of people, whilst a house known as St Philomena's has been extended to accommodate about two dozen people who are cared for by one of the monks, acting as guest-master, with the help of a warden and his wife.

At the monastery the food, both for visitors and monks, is prepared by members of the Community. The monks' diet, not normally including meat, can hardly be described as well-balanced, containing as it does, according to some authorities on the subject, too many carbohydrates. Like many other such matters of the world, this does not disturb the monks unduly and they manage to do a hard day's work on it.

Apart from the indoor work of baking, cooking, cleaning, washing and mending, all of which tasks are performed by those to whom they are allotted, there is much work to be done out-of-doors by way of gardening and keeping the whole place as tidy as possible, as well as the work in the revenue-producing enterprises. In addition to the boatmen and men employed on the farm, there is also one man employed on building maintenance, and for some time three were employed. Much of this work the monks would like to be doing themselves, but they do not have sufficient numbers in the Community for it to be possible. [*Numbers and circumstances have changed, and must inevitably continue to change from time to time, as for example with the invaluable help, already referred to, from the Friends of Caldey.*]

As the Rule of St Benedict says, 'If the needs of the place, or their poverty, oblige them to labour themselves at gathering in the crops let them not be saddened thereat, because then are they truly monks, when they live by the labour of their hands, as did our fathers and the Apostles.' To this end, possibly, the Abbot seeks to lead by example rather than precept and is frequently to be found performing all sorts of menial tasks. In the halcyon days of the annual visit of the coal boat he was always first on the job. When the village pond is in need of draining and cleaning, he tackles the foul-smelling task himself. It is nothing unusual to discover him washing floors, hoeing weeds, trimming grass or taking on a multiplicity of jobs which others have not had time to do.

The business affairs also involve various members of the Community in considerable paper work. To help with this an electronic accounting machine was recently installed. It did little to improve the monks' image when the press, radio and television reporters insisted on referring to it as a computer. The need for it, however, is just one more instance of how the monks, too, have to accept certain changes, especially in those spheres where they are of this world as well as in it. [*We now live in such an age when the press could make a meal of it if the monks did not have a computer. Not only has Br Robert (as he prefers to be called) followed in the footsteps of his predecessor in leading by example, but has also become something of a computer expert.*]

In the rationalisation of their own way of life, a significant change has come about in one of their customs, and that is concerning the burial of the dead.

When Br Thomas died in 1966 he was the first monk on Caldey to be buried in a coffin. Until that time it had been customary for a monk to be buried in his habit with one of the Brothers being down in the grave to receive the body. It was a custom rooted in mediaeval practice, when the coffin was associated with those wealthier classes who were able to afford such refinements. It was also a custom for Brothers to have to watch through the night with the corpse. Some of the younger members tended to find the whole procedure somewhat grisly, and the tradition was broken when Br Thomas died, because of the particular circumstances surrounding his sudden passing. It happened on a Saturday morning, and it was established that his body could be taken over to Tenby for a post-mortem and returned the same day, together with the necessary burial certificate. It was the height of the holiday season, and the conclusion was reached that the crowds thronging the harbour area would not care overmuch for the sight of 'a corpse being lugged about the place', as Fr Bernard put it. A coffin was therefore considered to be more proper to the occasion, even though this new custom is by no means popular with many of the Brothers, who believe that a coffin is a waste of money which would be better given to the poor. Except that they do not call it a coffin but a *box* and, in doing so, make it sound as disparaging as possible.

If any of the foregoing paragraph sounds in any way flippant or disrespectful, then it will not be out of keeping with the monks' attitude to death, which they regard, not as an end, but a beginning of something far greater. Fr Bernard was content to quote St Paul's letter to the Thessalonians when he wrote:

> I would not have you to be ignorant, brethren, concerning them which are asleep, that ye sorrow not, even as others which have no hope.
> For if we believe that Jesus died and rose again, even so them also which sleep in Jesus will God bring with him.
> And then he added, 'All this business of flowers and coffins and that sort of thing is a lot of nonsense for the sake of the living. The tears are all for the living. For the dead it is a joyful event ready to lead on to greater things.'

Perhaps the biggest change of all, however, is in the lead which is being given by the Abbot towards Christian unity. When the Cistercians came to Caldey, the concern of the Bishop of Menevia, when he sent his telegram of good wishes, was that this new foundation should ultimately be the means of bringing the whole country back to Holy Church. Now, more than half-a-century later, such change has there been in thinking in many places that we see a brave attempt being made by that same foundation in the infinitely more important task of bringing the world back to Christ.

17
DIFFERENT BELIEFS AND
ATTEMPTS AT UNITY

'Let your light so shine before men, that they may see your good works, and glorify your Father which is in Heaven':
Matthew 5:16

Throughout the years the divisions between Churches and denominations have been deep and sometimes bitter. Yet these same divisions are bound to become less important to the thinking followers of any of the various creeds in face of the certain knowledge that the whole of Christianity has a common enemy. Whether the Church be Orthodox, Catholic or Protestant, it has to live in a secular age where materialism is the false god most readily worshipped.

Dom James Wicksteed gave a lead in the Tenby area by inviting leaders of the various denominations to a united service on Caldey. He, in turn, took an active part in united efforts on the mainland, and represented the Churches of the area, as well as his own Church, on the Committee of the Wales for Christ Movement. Whilst it would be idle to pretend that the movement has yet shown any signs of sweeping the country like an all-consuming flame, it is an encouraging pointer.

Of recent years, after a long struggle on the part of forward-thinking people, the majority of the English Congregationalists in Wales joined with the English Presbyterians to form the United Reformed Church, and some of the ecumenically-minded leaders of this movement have already held retreats on Caldey, and been welcomed there, for mutual study of problems which should be exercising the minds of Christians everywhere.

There is, of course, nothing new in this division and dissent. In his letters to the Churches at Rome, Corinth and Ephesus, Paul had much to say on the subject, and was constantly reminding them that they were all members of one body. Long before that, way back where it all began, Jesus had to take his disciples to task because they had been disputing among themselves along the way as to who should be the greatest among them. Apart from the occasional zealot, however, I have usually found that criticism of the Catholics as often as not comes from those who rarely attend any place of worship, but describe themselves as C. of E. on application forms where religion has to be declared, whilst being content to be known as 'outside pillars'.

Perhaps this comes from sheer prejudice, or even from the constant pricking of a guilty conscience, because I realised as I grew older and thought about things for myself that, however black the Catholics had been painted, they are generally active and sincere about their religion. Then I began to understand that they had retained the Hebrew genius for seeing the divine in the common things of life, for seeing the burning bush everywhere and making religion something for everyday. And this genius was evident as far back as Deuteronomy:

> Hear, O Israel: the Lord our God is one Lord:
> And thou shalt love the Lord thy God with all thine heart, and with all thy soul, and with all thy might.
> And these words, which I command thee this day, shall be in thine heart.
> And thou shalt teach them diligently unto thy children, and shalt talk of them when thou sittest in thine house, and when thou walkest by the way, and when thou liest down, and when thou risest up.
> And thou shalt bind them for a sign upon thine head, and they shall be as frontlets between thine eyes.
> And thou shalt write them upon the posts of thy house, and on thy gates.

Remembering this, I found it easier to understand the Catholics.' preoccupation with what I had been taught was mumbo-jumbo. A crucifix upon the wall is no more than a constant reminder. The symbolic act of crossing themselves dates from the time when Christians were persecuted and needed to make some sort of sign to identify each other, and using beads during prayer dates from the days when the illiterate could not count or read, and used the beads as an aid.

There then came a time when I wanted to know what purgatory was all about, and where was the Gospel authority for such a belief. I shall make no attempt to try to explain it as Catholics have explained it to me, but must confess that it sounded quite feasible and acceptable. I found nothing in it to lead me to fear that my Nonconformist soul was in mortal danger, or that I was coming under the dread influence of some great evil, by consorting with those for whom it was a necessary belief. If indeed there is this purgatory as a place of spiritual cleansing for the dead, then we know we have the assurance that, 'In my Father's house are many mansions: if it were not so, I would have told you.'

There are, no doubt, many counts on which the Roman Catholic Church can be criticised. No man in his right mind could attempt to justify the horrors of the Inquisition, because we have now advanced to a stage where toleration is widely accepted. So perhaps it should be seen in the context of the thinking of its own age, an age that was responsible for many great social evils. Then again there has been the political intrigue in which the Roman Catholic Church has been involved, and the interference in the private lives of people.

Is the Anglican Church, however, proud of the part it played in the slave trade? Would anyone still try to justify the sign which was displayed in our own parish church when I was a boy, telling the poorer people where to sit, well back out of the way of the gentlefolk who had paid for their seats?

It is not perhaps too much to hope that some Nonconformist of today will not feel too proud of the actions and attitude of the not-so-long-ago when unfortunate girls were called before the congregation and hounded out of chapel in shame. Nor can some of them have won many followers for Christ with their narrow stiff-necked, wing-collared bigotry, turning places of worship into empty timber-yards where, instead of the compassion which Christ constantly preached, the only real belief seemed to be in 'all for misery and misery for all'.

It is now four and a half centuries since Martin Luther, a monk of vast intellect, started the Reformation. Yet he remained a Catholic in much of his thinking until the end. It was the tyranny and the corruption to which he was mainly opposed.

Basically, Luther propounded the belief that man is justified by faith alone, whereas the Catholic believes, and there are abundant gospel justifications for it, that good works can help a good man towards salvation. Now, however, on so many issues, the same sharp division between Catholics and Protestants no longer exists. In both camps there are the evangelicals who claim to have been 'saved', whilst amongst themselves they also differ on certain fundamentals. Even the Catholics are divided on certain issues.

I had experience of this after starting work on this book. Although I had been visiting Caldey for many years, it was not until I had begun this work that I had occasion to stay on the Island. I went there for the week-end when the monks would have more time to be able to talk to me. Whilst it was far from my mind to go to Church seven times a day, and still less to get up at quarter-past-three in the morning, I thought I ought to make the gesture, if only out of courtesy, and put in an appearance at one of the services. After due consultation it was decided that eleven o'clock Mass on the Sunday morning would be the most suitable service for me to attend. Not knowing anything of the routine, and going into Church from the Monastery side, since that was where I was staying, I found myself in the choir stalls with the monks, like some 'latter-day Harry Worth', in full view of the village community who were seated upstairs in the gallery.

This, however, was not the greatest of my problems. My real concern came as that part of the service was approaching when the sacraments were to be taken, for I just did not know either what to do for the best, or what would be expected of me. I knew that in the Anglican Church they do not expect to give Communion to those who have not been confirmed. In chapel, when Communion is being celebrated, the Secretary, in his announcements, invites visitors who 'love the Lord Jesus Christ' to join in fellowship round the table. But what the Catholics felt about the matter, bearing in mind the predicament in which I found myself, I had no idea. If I went forward in turn with the others, would the Abbot be put in the embarrassing position of having to refuse me? On the other hand, if I made no move, would it look as if I did not wish to take part in the most sacred rite of any Christian service and thereby, however unwittingly, give offence?

In the event, I did nothing but, as soon as possible afterwards, I took the opportunity of explaining to some of the monks how

I had felt. To my surprise, there was a complete difference of opinion amongst them as to whether or not they would have given me Communion. Some said that, in the circumstances, they would definitely have given me Communion, whilst others said they did not think *rapprochement* had yet gone far enough for them to have felt able to do so.

There are other issues on which Catholics are currently divided, and it causes some of them deep concern. Birth control is one such issue. Nor can many Catholics see any good reason why priests should be celibate, since the rule is a legacy of the monastic days when monks became priests. And only the most conservative amongst Catholics would now flaunt their belief in the infallibility of the Pope, other than when he is speaking *ex-cathedra*.

It is, too, perhaps worth mentioning that, contrary to many people's ideas, the monks have many employees who are not Catholics. What is more, not only is no pressure put upon them, but the approach is never even made. If, as has happened on the odd occasion, an employee or tenant should choose to become a convert, it has no more significance than if it should happen to anyone else.

To come back, however, to the Mass where I found myself in something of a dilemma. Before Communion came the exchange of the 'kiss of peace', and immediately following this I was deeply conscious of something, a Presence or moving of the Spirit, or whatever it may be called. My charismatic friends would no doubt like me to recognise that in that moment I was saved. That has often struck me as being one of the failings with the over-enthusiastic, who insist that you have to see things their way. As Gerard W. Hughes, a Jesuist priest, has written in his lovely book, *God of Surprises*, 'No religion can monopolize God, although most of them will try to do so, claiming that unless you follow their particular way, you cannot be saved.'

The 'kiss of peace', of course, is there in the Scriptures with the early Christians, and it was refreshing recently to hear a Nonconformist preacher, instead of condemning the beliefs of other denominations, saying it was a pity our founding fathers had cut themselves off from some of the good things of the Church, such as the observance of Lent. It is no bad thing to have habits if they are good habits. Nor is it perhaps any bad thing, in an age of uncertainty, to have some doctrines of certainty.

It is difficult to believe, however, that Christians can afford to dissipate their energies in arguing about those points on which they disagree when there are so many issues on which there is no disagreement, and when the real enemy is seen to be materialism, secular living and society's complete disregard for the individual. The real issue is Christianity itself. Not whether it is believable, but whether it is possible, for Christianity is something not merely to be believed, but to be lived. It is a question which can never be settled by argument, but only by example. As the Apostle James wrote in his brief Epistle— 'Shew me thy faith without works, and I will shew thee my faith by my works.'

18
FUTURE PROSPECTS

'Be of good courage, and he shall strengthen your heart, all ye that hope in the Lord': Psalms 31:24

The two previous monastic settlements on Caldey each lasted for four centuries.

The present Cistercian foundation has a long way to go to catch up with that sort of record, and life now, and certainly in the future, is, and will be, moving and changing at a far greater rate than could ever have been dreamed of by those earlier Communities. What the future holds, and whether the monks can meet its challenge, must remain to be seen, and can only be a matter for conjecture. As will have been seen in these pages, the challenge will come under the two main headings of *spiritual* and *secular*.

Commercially, the monks would seem now to have organised their affairs very well, but still have, and always will have, problems to sort out. Overall, they will no doubt have to make sure they avoid the danger of specialising in any one venture simply because it seems to be more profitable at the time.

The tourist trade, for example, has made in the past a considerable contribution to the Island's economy, but it would be foolish to rely on it exclusively because, apart from the many monastic and other considerations, in time of war or national crisis it could collapse overnight. Likewise, in the case of the successful perfume industry, there is the dependence on essential ingredients now being imported from all over the world. For any one or more of a multitude of reasons beyond the monks' control, some or all of these supplies could cease completely, and the entire economy of the Island, if relying on the perfume, be put in jeopardy.

Apart from the basic consideration that agriculture, according to their Rule, is part of the Cistercians' way of life, it would be an act of lunacy to abandon or neglect the farm, as was seen by the nation after years of betrayal of its farmers preceding two world wars. Because there are no signs that the country has even yet learned its lesson is no reason to advocate that the monks should make the same mistake.

The farming pattern on the Island in the future will no doubt vary and have to be changed and modified from time to time as circumstances dictate. The sheep flock, with four hundred breeding ewes, remains at the basis for a sound farming system, but the pigs have been disposed of in favour of a dairy policy which would not have been possible when the idea was first mooted. With the advent of the European Community the price structure of milk has been changed, and it has become possible for manufacturing milk to earn something nearer its real worth. The Jersey herd has been built up to forty cows, with their milk going into cream, yoghurt, butter and soft cheese. Modern yoghurt is a consumer development of recent years and was not a possible solution to the challenge in Fr Anthony's day.

Originally it had been intended to make hard cheeses, but this would not have been possible with Jersey milk, because the fat globules are too big. This quality product, however, is ideal for making butter. The difficulty in this case is the profitable disposal of the skim or separated milk. In the absence of pigs to which this could be fed, the yoghurt is an ideal outlet. Some of these products can be sold direct to the public through the monks' own shops, but other markets also have to be found, and the ability to produce milk to be made into butter will in the end depend on the ability to sell yoghurt. In other words, unless the skim milk can be disposed of successfully, in this case by making yoghurt and selling it, the butter would provide too small a return on its own for the operation to be worthwhile.

In turn, the farm itself is restricted in its output by the ability of the dairy enterprise to find a market for its products. The farm is capable of carrying a much larger herd of cows, but this is of no help unless the dairy enterprise can find markets for the milk in the form of the yoghurt, butter, cream and cheese. Considerable capital has had to be invested in dairy equipment and cold storage plant, but it was the only way the problem could be tackled. Most of the other possibilities have been discussed in these pages and seem to be non-viable for any island farmer in the context of a modern economy. Certainly in face of competition from the supermarket and the deep freeze, the growth and sale of fresh vegetables would seem to be a less attractive proposition than ever. About the only idea not yet discussed is a beef unit with a slaughterhouse. Like everything else it would need much thought.

Some barley is still being grown for sale, and a reasonable system, using specially-made crates, has been evolved for transporting it to the mainland, thirty hundredweights at a time. It is useful, but can never be competitive in the push-button age of automation. The 'Ducks' are still used occasionally, mainly for getting people ashore when the tide goes out too far for the jetty on the Island to be used, but their uses otherwise have been found to be strictly limited.

One great advantage Caldey farming now enjoys is that, for the first time for nearly seven centuries, the Island at last seems to be clear of rabbits. The rabbit population on other islands has crashed dramatically on various occasions since 1954 as the result of myxomatosis, but each time the numbers have built up again very quickly from the few survivors, with no stoats, weasels, foxes or badgers to keep them down. On Caldey, however, every effort has been made to seek out and destroy the survivors, and there has been no sign of rabbits there for some time.

In addition to these main enterprises there are a few side-lines bringing in some revenue. These include the making of chocolate and cakes, and the polishing and setting of stones for necklaces by Br James, who is a keen archaeologist. He has done much digging in some of the Island's caves, and has made a number of interesting discoveries.

As with the perfume, the monks have the considerable benefit of being able to sell these products in their own shops, thereby cutting out the middleman. They have two shops on the Island and two on the mainland, one of which is in Tenby and one in neighbouring Saundersfoot. At one time they also had a shop in London, but this was given up when the lease expired.

Having direct access to the customer made possible by the possession of these shops has, however, led the monks into a commercial situation which gives rise to one area of doubt, both on grounds of ethics and good management, because a considerable trade has now developed in the sale of all manner of souvenirs made specially for the monks by outside people.

This means that, in this sphere, they have become traders rather than producers. Whilst, as producers, they are completely justified in trying to sell their wares in the best possible market, there cannot be the same monastic justification for setting up as traders. There is plenty of bric-a-brac available for tourists in the Persian market of the seaside areas, without any obvious need for the monks to become a part of it. And, from the point-of-view of sound business, it is perhaps arguable whether the return justifies the extra labour required to cope with it. Here again is another example of the difficulty of keeping the balance between monastic ideals and financial prudence. It is all too easy for a monastic business venture to become so big as to overshadow the monasticism itself, as happened at Aiguebelle in France where the chocolate business, started by the monks, developed to such an extent that it was eventually sold.

[*Note.—Inevitably, since this was written twenty years ago, there have been many changes, in the farming in particular. Much of it has been recorded in my other two books,* Caldey *and* Farewell the Islands. *Now, as then, it is impossible to anticipate with certainty what changes are still to come. The sheep flock, for the time being at any rate, has been disposed of. If the Island is to be farmed successfully, sheep, those creatures of the 'golden hoof', will have to be reintroduced one day. It can be confirmed now that rabbits really have been exterminated at last, and this is a colossal bonus. The shop in Saundersfoot has been sold. Br James, who had been 'on loan' from Chimay for more than forty years, has returned there at last, so there is no more polishing of stones. But Fr Richard does wood-turning and his products are sold.—R.H.*]

So, then, whatever steps have to be taken in the light of changing conditions to ensure the monks' financial survival on Caldey, it remains to be seen what the future holds for them in their vocation spiritually. Arguments as to the worth of that vocation to the world are as old as the hills. But, as Paul wrote to the Corinthians, 'There are diversities of gifts, but the same Spirit.' And, later in the same chapter:

> God hath set some in the Church, first apostles, secondarily prophets, thirdly teachers, after that miracles, then gifts of healings, helps, governments, diversity of tongues.

Are all apostles? are all prophets? are all teachers? are all workers
of miracles?
Have all the gifts of healing? do all speak with tongues? do all
interpret?
But covet earnestly the best gifts: and yet I shew unto you a more
excellent way.

Paul was writing to the Church leaders. If he were writing to
society today he could ask what would happen if we were all to
be farmers, or callers in bingo halls, croupiers in gambling
saloons, doctors, writers, parsons, bookmakers, public-house
pianists, footballers, road-sweepers, miners, or any one of
hundreds of occupations, the followers of which are doing
what they want to do and are convinced that they are making
a contribution to the society in or on which they live?

Peter Anson, who gave me so much valuable help with the
first two chapters of this book, was interviewed for a newspaper
feature in 1971, and much prominence was given to his
somewhat gloomy prophecy that monasticism on Caldey was
doomed. Mr Anson, however, whilst being a world authority
on monastic history, was not necessarily an authority on
monasticism. Although he was a member of the Benedictine
Community on Caldey at different times between 1910 and
1924, he never did come to terms with the monastic life or take
his vows. In later years he recognised that it was probably his
love of the sea which had drawn him there in the first place.
This love of the sea manifested itself in the way he earned his
living, with a gifted paint-brush and a fluent pen, amongst
seagoing people, and he was one of the founders of the
Apostleship of the Sea. He remained remarkably active
physically, and keenly alert mentally, until his death at
Nunraw, in July 1975, at the age of eighty-six, when this work
had just been completed.

It will always be one of my regrets that he was unable to read
it, because he was so enthusiastic about the intention of it and
gave me so much encouragement.

There are those, however, committed to the monastic life,
who have no qualms about the future. It is true, of course, that
in recent years Caldey, in common with most other religious
communities, has suffered from a serious falling-off in recruit-

ment. However, there are now firm indications that the tide is beginning to turn again, and this gives the Community grounds for quiet optimism.

For those who feel truly called to it, it is a good life with its own rewards. There are not many vocations which people can follow without ever feeling the need of a holiday. Whatever its detractors may say, monasticism can still offer hope to a materialistic world where there is so much lack of balance, and help it to retain its sanity. The monastic idea will always be there, and men will decide for themselves whether and how they will use it.

For my own part I would only say that writing this book has proved to be a most rewarding experience. If I have succeeded in helping towards a little better understanding in a world where there is so much room for a more charitable outlook by man towards his fellow-man, then it will have been even more worthwhile.

ABBAYE N.-D. DE SCOURMONT

B - 6483 FORGES (Belgique)

Tél : 060/211545   Jan. 27, 1976

Dear Mr. Howells,

Your book on the Community of Caldey is really a remarkable
account of the life, persons and events of this community
since its departure from Chimay, nearly 50 years ago.

I must say I read it with great interest . You give an
excellent idea, pertinent and well balanced, of the many
difficulties of this fondation. The economival problem
is set in the wider scope of general farming of the time
and the country; this context explains many failures and
hardships.

I appreciate your discretion, but also your perspicacity
in dealing with the documents of archives. Remembering
this history, more particularly the portion of it in
which I had been involved, in difficult circumstances,
I was struck by the abondance of informations , yet the
elegant sobriety with which you avoid the modern sensation-
alism of the kind of the journalists you have exposed in
some funny pages of the book.

As abbot of Scourmont I thank you for the appreciative
judgement on the persons belonging to our community and
on their contribution to maintain Caldey above water.

Many pictures were unknown to me , I was amused by some
and touched by others, as by that last photo of Bro Thomas.

I congratulate you, Mr Howells, on the success of this
book; I thank you for your love of Caldey, and I assure
you of my gratitude for the enjoyment I had reading it.

                Your sincerely

Mr Roscoe Howells

Letter from Dom Guerric Baudet, Abbot of N. D. De Scourmont,
received by the author following publication of the first edition, and
published with his permission.